PRAISE FOR *THE ELEGANT WARRIOR*

"*The Elegant Warrior* pairs extraordinary stories from inside the courtroom with actionable advice to use outside the courtroom. By applying the tools successful lawyers use to your own challenges, you'll find the evidence that proves you're a winner and a warrior."

MEL ROBBINS, author of the international bestseller *The 5 Second Rule*

"If you want to better advocate for yourself—in business and in life—Heather Hansen's insights in *The Elegant Warrior* will prove invaluable."

DORIE CLARK, adjunct professor at Duke University's Fuqua School of Business and author of *Entrepreneurial You* and *Stand Out*

"With insight, wonderful examples, and a strong motivational voice, Heather Hansen provides a beacon for women who want to create a life of unique meaning and purpose. She doesn't promise the path will be easy but, like the words of a true friend whispered in your ear, her encouragement will make your journey rewarding."

LOIS P. FRANKEL, PhD, author of *Nice Girls Don't Get the Corner Office*

"In *The Elegant Warrior*, Hansen reminds us that we must maintain both a warrior side and an elegant side. Her stories help the reader understand how finding that balance is a constant battle. I urge you to read *The Elegant Warrior* and adjust your dial as required!"

LIANE DAVEY, bestselling author of *You Fir*

"Motivational, meaningful, powerful messages. Heather Hansen is *the* Elegant Warrior who liberates the Elegant Warrior carried inside each of us. Inspirational stories that demonstrate superior outcomes result with the right approach, attitude, and mind-set. Readers are enriched with learning tools for effective, positive results, in all aspects of their life. A must-read!"

ROSEMARIE E. AQUILINA, 30th Circuit Court Judge, *Vanity Fair*'s 2018 Hall of Fame and *Glamour*'s 2018 Woman of the Year recipient

"Inspiring and original. With captivating grace and insight with a sprinkling of humor, Heather guides and probes us to question and consider our decisions on our life's journey."

LIZANN BOYLE RODE, executive director, alumni relations, The Wharton School

THE
ELEGANT
WARRIOR

HOW TO WIN
LIFE'S TRIALS WITHOUT
LOSING YOURSELF

HEATHER HANSEN

THE
ELEGANT
Warrior

PAGE TWO
BOOKS

Cataloguing in publication information is
available from Library and Archives Canada.
ISBN 978-1-989025-26-0 (paperback)
ISBN 978-1-989025-76-5 (ebook)

Page Two Books
www.pagetwo.com

Cover design by Peter Cocking
Interior design by Setareh Ashrafologhalai & Peter Cocking
Printed and bound in Canada by Friesens
Distributed in Canada by Raincoast Books
Distributed in the US and internationally by
Publishers Group West, a division of Ingram

19 20 21 22 23   5 4 3 2 1

www.heatherhansenpresents.com

To Mum and Dad—

I'm everything I am because you loved me

Contents

INTRODUCTION
Choose Your Elegance

"We are our choices."
JEAN-PAUL SARTRE

I HELD BACK THE tears until I made it to my car. I could feel them rising, hot and tight in my throat, as I stood in the courtroom. But a woman can't cry in court, not if she's a trial lawyer, and especially if, like me, she's a medical malpractice defense lawyer.

Many of my cases involve catastrophic injuries, dead mothers, paralyzed lovers, babies on feeding tubes with muscles so contracted that their whole bodies seem to be grimacing. Those people have reason to cry. We cry when we feel sadness, anger, frustration, and joy. In my work, there are always reasons to cry. But compared to those injured patients', a lawyer's reasons are trivial.

My mother is a crier, and so was her mother. It may be that I learned to cry by watching them, or maybe tears are in my blood, mixed up with the platelets and blood cells. It doesn't matter so much where they come from, nature or nurture; what matters is where they go. And when I'm trying a case and advocating for my client, they can't go anywhere that people might see them. Certainly not in the courtroom.

On those days when I lost a case, my tears threatened to erupt. Fortunately for me and my clients, I can count on one hand the number of cases I've lost—but the tears I've cried over those losses filled many handfuls of tissues. And trial lawyers have other losses. We can lose at arbitration, we can lose arguments, we can lose clients. Like you, we also experience losses outside our workplace—we can lose friends, lovers, and time. My saltiest tears have been from the times I've lost my way.

On that day when I escaped the courtroom without crying, my Toyota RAV4 became my valley of tears. I felt lost. I'd been practicing for twenty years. I'd started at my firm when I was in law school, taking every opportunity I had to go to trial with my mentor and uncle, John. I'd tried hundreds of cases, playing every role from questioning the most minor of witnesses, to standing before the jury with the weight of the entire case on my shoulders. My car had seen a lot of tears; this time, they were personal.

The case involved a young man. He'd been in pain when he first met my client, a doctor, in the emergency room. He'd been in pain for years prior to ever laying eyes on my doctor, and he was still in pain. When he'd come to the emergency room, his pain was in his chest. He'd been taking medications for years, both for his pain and for his anxiety. He claimed he told my doctor he was taking large amounts of a pain medication. My client, Dr. S, documented and specifically remembered that the patient had been taking a small amount of this medication, so Dr. S ordered a small amount to be administered in the hospital. It wasn't enough, and the young man had a withdrawal seizure that broke his arm and gave him a concussion. He sued.

Before lawyers go to court, we take depositions. Depositions are where we explore the stories that will be told to the judge and the jury; speaking directly to the plaintiff, defendant, and witnesses, asking questions to explore those stories, and collecting facts we will later use at trial. During the depositions of the patients who sue my doctors, I explore the truth of their allegations.

This young man had a sad story. He had cystic fibrosis, a condition that caused him physical pain, but his suffering didn't seem to me to be purely physical. This patient had a lot that hurt, and his pain was obvious on his face and in his eyes. I felt bad for him, and I liked him. During the deposition he was sick with anxiety, and he had to go to the bathroom a number of times before we even started the process. Since he wasn't a trial lawyer or a defendant, it was okay for him to cry, and cry he did. He cried before I even asked him a question. But we had to proceed, and soon after we began, he told me he'd feel better if he wasn't wearing his boots. They were Timberland boots, stiff and unyielding, and he couldn't get them off, so I got down on the floor to untie them. With his lawyer looking on, unsure what to do, I pulled, he pushed with his opposite foot, and together we laughed as the boots popped off. And then I got back to work, asking questions, probing for evidence that I could use to argue my case when we got to trial.

Many months later, it was time for trial. We tried the case for a week. Every morning I greeted the patient and his family, and every day at the end of the lunch break he offered me a mint. This may have been kindness, or it may have been manipulation. From where I sat it seemed that his family had fallen victim to his charms, and I worried the jury would, too. I knew the patient's lawyer was saving him as his last witness, a strategic move meant to leave the jury with sympathy at the end of his case. I liked him, but I had to cross-examine him because I believed he was lying.

He didn't make it easy. Right before he went up to testify, he introduced me to his mother. "This is the lawyer I told you about," he said. "The one who was so nice to me and helped me with my shoes." It's hard to prepare for war when your opponent's mother is tearfully thanking you for being nice. But trials are battles, and I am a warrior.

I put on my armor, and I tore this young man's story apart. His timing didn't make sense. His story was inconsistent with the medical record created at the time. He was contradicting not only my doctor, but also the nurses who had written in the record. It was my job to slowly and painstakingly show the jury the inconsistencies, to prove him a liar. I might be nice, but I had a job to do. And I was good at it. I killed him on cross-examination. He said he'd told the nurses all of his medications, and I showed him (and the jury) each and every time in the medical record where he had left medications out of his list. He said he'd never been questioned about drug-seeking behavior, and I showed him other hospitalizations where the medical providers documented those conversations with him. One by one, piece of evidence by piece of evidence, I showed the jury his lies. And I did it with a smile.

But the smile masked my own distress. On this day, after the cross-examination, I cried tears of confusion in my RAV4. Was I remaining true to who I was, and who I wanted to be? Was that even possible in times of trial? I had a job to do, a client to protect, a fight to win. But I wanted to be kind and compassionate. I wanted us all to win. I knew that wasn't possible, so I wanted to be sure I was elegant in victory and graceful in defeat.

Dr. S and I won that case. The jury wanted to speak to Dr. S after the verdict, and they told him they appreciated his kindness, his compassion, and the care he rendered. They lauded my hard work and my arguments but made no mention of my empathy or my compassion. A warrior isn't often commended for her heart.

In my twenty years of practice, I've had many successes. I've been named one of the Top 50 female lawyers in Pennsylvania and been inducted into the American College of Trial Lawyers. But I wanted to be sure that what it took to win hadn't forced me to lose myself, my dignity, my elegance.

My grandmother, the same one who may have passed on the tendency to cry, also gave me a love of elegance. *Merriam-Webster* defines *elegance* as a "refined grace," and my grandmother was elegant both in the way she looked and the way she acted. For years she'd been a social worker, working outside the home long before that was the norm for women. In that role, she'd been able to use her innate kindness and ability to talk to people. Even when rushing through the hospital to work with the patients she'd been assigned, high heels clicking down the halls, she never had a hair out of place. Throughout the hospital she was known for her kindness, her smile, and the fact that she always wore earrings and lipstick.

She expected the same from me, even from an early age. I lived with her during the summers while I waitressed at the Chart Room, a well-known Cape Cod restaurant. When I'd leave for work, in my denim skirt and orange apron, I'd go upstairs to kiss her good-bye. She'd give me her wrinkled cheek and determine whether I passed muster. Her expectations were earrings, lipstick, compassion, and grace. How hard could that be? I've come to learn that makeup and jewelry are just the props, and true elegance gets much harder from there.

Earrings and lipstick are easy, but they're not the hallmark of true elegance. The word *elegance* comes from the Latin *eligo* which means "to choose." You choose your way to elegance, and you choose how to fight your wars. But you have to be aware that you're making a choice. It has to be conscious. By choosing rather than allowing, you shift from a victim mentality to a warrior mentality. In order to win in all areas of life without losing yourself, you have to make that choice, and make it with intent.

THE ELEGANT WARRIOR

Elegance is available to men and women, baby boomers and millennials. It is the ability to be true to yourself, both who you are and who you feel destined to be, no matter what inner and outer wars you face. And elegance often has to be chosen in the heat of battle. I didn't realize what a challenge this choice could be until my first trial. In the courtroom I could maintain the earrings, and reapply the lipstick, but my compassion had to be tempered with a fighting spirit, and my grace had to be countered with a willingness to go in for the kill in defense of my client. Elegance feels like one thing; being a warrior feels like another. When we strive for both, we often miss the mark. It's tempting to give up on the balance and to go for the win like a warrior; or to give up the fight, with elegance—but with awareness and presence you can have both. You can look to Maya Angelou, Atticus Finch, Mary Oliver, Laura Bush, and Oprah Winfrey as examples.

You might not be a lawyer, but you have trials. You have battles that you have to fight, and you want to win. Sometimes those battles are personal, defending who and what you love. Sometimes they're professional. At times, they're both. After years of fighting battles inside and outside the courtroom, I know that it's possible to win our battles with elegance. We can be warriors without losing our grace or our compassion. We can respect ourselves and others while we fight. We can win life's trials without losing ourselves. And we don't need to put on earrings or lipstick to PROVE IT. You can win your battles without losing your own personal elegance, whatever that means to you.

Everything I know about being an Elegant Warrior I've learned in the courtroom. Lawyers ask questions and give voice to objections—these are two of our key tools. In this book, I will share these and other essential tools I've used to succeed in the courtroom. We call our tales from the courtroom "war stories," and the rooms where we prepare for trial "war rooms." You also have war stories and war rooms, be they the bedroom, the boardroom, or the operating room. No matter your battle-field, you can use these tools, too—with your loved ones, your colleagues, and especially with yourself.

I believe there are two ways to have the tallest building in town: you can build it, or you can knock down everyone else's building. In the courtroom, I have to do both. I build my case and my credibility with evidence. However, sometimes my job is to knock the other side down by attacking the evidence they use to build their cases. In life, you have similar choices. You get the chance to build, and your foundation will be the choices you make. You also get the chance to destroy, when the situation calls for it. But most of the time, outside of the courtroom, there is room for compromise. The great thing about life's trials is that most of them aren't a zero-sum game.

WHAT TO EXPECT

The law is nice and orderly. Life is not. So while this book is laid out to follow the order of a typical lawsuit and trial, your battles will be far less organized. That's okay. Take what you need and leave the rest.

Each chapter focuses on a different aspect of the law or how I approached a trial, and the lesson it taught me. But as I tell my juries, you don't have to take my word for it. My job is to prove my cases with evidence. I will do the same for you, ending each chapter with scientific evidence to back up my claims. And then I'll give you a short Summary of the Case—because let's face it, you're busy, just like judges. Most judges I know have law clerks who read our briefs before they do, and those law clerks tend to go right to the Summary of the Case. Since you'll be the judge of my book, I want to give you the same option.

You all put on armor to fight your battles. Yours might be your sense of humor, your smile, your sarcasm, or your preparation. After reading this book, you will have more weapons to add to your arsenal. Let these lessons from lawsuits be your tools when you need to be a warrior, elegant in whatever way feels right to you.

1

Don't Just Complain—Move

*"The only thing complaining does is convince
other people that you aren't in control."*
ANONYMOUS

SOMETIMES YOU FIND yourself surrounded by complaints.
I've found that the best thing to do in those situations is
to move, and perhaps even to sing. A complaint without
movement will get you nowhere.

When I was in high school, I was about one hundred pounds
overweight. In general, I was happy, but I wanted to lose weight
and there were days when I cried about not going to prom, not
having a boyfriend, and feeling like I was missing out. There
were times I'd complain, but not often. More often than not,
you'd find me singing. I just liked to sing.

One day, I was in the girls' bathroom, putting on my new
Clinique Black Honey lip gloss, and I thought I was alone so
I was quietly singing. While I don't have a good voice, that
lack has never stopped me from singing in the car, at home,

and anywhere I don't think someone will hear. But there was someone in the last stall, and she came out with a look of disdain. I waited for her to make fun of me, my voice, or my choice of song (Broadway musical, not pop rock). Instead she said, "What do you have to be so happy about?"

The question stopped me in my tracks. I saw what she saw—a teenage girl with no boyfriend, uncomfortable in her own skin and in the clothes she'd bought at Lane Bryant, a clothing store for plus-size women. I didn't know how to answer her question. What *did* I have to be so happy about? And the bigger question for me was, did I sing because I was happy or was I happy because I sang? Would complaining about my situation make things better or worse? I saw myself from her perspective, and I didn't like what I saw. So I chose not to stay there.

I lost the weight in college, gained some boyfriends, and years later I was a lawyer, sitting at a desk covered with a pile of complaints and a Dictaphone. My job was to answer the complaints, those legal filings that start a civil lawsuit. Spending all of that time surrounded by complaints took its toll. My perspective had changed and I had stopped singing and started complaining. But I found the more I complained, the more I found to complain about.

Soon, though, I discovered that complaints weren't fatal. They were just the beginning, the first step in the resolution of a lawsuit. In my cases the complaint had to be dealt with, and that meant something had to move. A complaint had to be followed by discovery, questions, exploration. If I stopped with the complaint, nothing happened. Nothing changed, and there was no opportunity to see things from another perspective. But once I started moving, new ideas showed themselves and I could see the complaints in a different way. Movement changes perspective.

The same is true for you. If you surround yourself with complaints, complaints are all you can see. You need to move to see past them. Sometimes that means leaving your seat and stepping outside to take a walk and look at the complaint in a new way. Other times, it means leaving a relationship that is no longer supporting your growth. It can also mean something as simple as picking up the vacuum rather than complaining about the dirty floor. Movement changes things.

I often think back to that moment in the bathroom. What did I have to be so happy about? Nothing, I guess. But I was the type of child who chose to be happy, and that in itself is something to celebrate. I saw songs where I could have seen complaints, and made the decision to sing. Later, as a lawyer, that way of looking at the world helped me to dig out of the pile of complaints that could have weighed me down. You can see the world as full of complaints, or full of song. Remember, though, sometimes your perspective depends on where you are standing. Move, and things can change.

PROVE IT

For most of us, complaining may actually cause more stress. And the more you complain, the more inclined you are to complain. Our brains create pathways, and by complaining you are creating more and more "complaining pathways." You can think of these pathways as ruts, if you prefer—you can get stuck in one way of thinking. If you're stuck in a rut that causes stress, you may actually be shrinking the hippocampus, the part of the brain that involves memory and learning.[1] When you move out of that rut, you can create a different pathway and gain a different perspective.

SUMMARY OF THE CASE

1. Complaints are one way of looking at things. They're one perspective. When you move, you have the opportunity to see them differently.

2. When you're surrounded by complaints, it's easy to get into the rut of complaining. Once you find your power and move, the change in perspective can change everything.

3. Recognize your complaints for what they are: a call to action. Complain when you must, but don't forget to move.

2

Discover Your
Personal Elegance

*"I think that somehow, we learn who we really
are and then we live with that decision."*

ELEANOR ROOSEVELT

IN LAWSUITS, DISCOVERY is the process through which
you indulge your curiosity, ask questions, and find treasure.
Discovery can do the same for you in your own life. Elegance
is personal, and it's based upon your goals and needs. Only you
can know what choices you need to make to find your elegance,
and those choices will change with time and circumstance. One
thing is for sure: you will never know your individual elegance if
you don't ask questions. Then the process of discovery involves
being brave enough to follow the answers where they lead.

The Honorable Sandra Mazer Moss is a retired judge in Philadelphia. For years, I tried cases before her. Her personal look
of elegance has included lots of jewelry, stylish suits, and a perfectly done hairstyle. But I recently learned this wasn't always

the case. Judge Moss found her personal style and place in the world through a process of discovery. She was a female lawyer at a time where that was rare, and a single mom which made her story even more unusual. Early in her legal career, she worked at the City of Philadelphia's Solicitor's office, the only woman in an army of men. Judge Moss became a warrior, for sure, but her elegance was kept under wraps. She loved jewelry, makeup, and beautiful clothes, but she wore drab, conservative dark suits to fit in with the men around her.

But that all changed with one seminal event. Judge Moss was asked to chair a panel at a bar conference, with a cocktail party to follow. She wore yet another conservative suit for the panel, her camouflage, but she also brought her precious jewelry and her beautiful dress to wear to the cocktail party. The panel discussion was lauded as one of the best the attendees had ever seen. Sandra Moss was on a high as she headed up to her room to change into her jewels and her dress. But they were gone, stolen.

Judge Moss decided to see the theft as a valuable gift, even a sign. Never again would she attempt to fit another's vision of how she should dress, look, or act. She would decide what worked for her, and not keep her true self hidden away. Ever since, Judge Moss has been known for her jewelry, and especially her brooches. With the loss of that jewelry, she discovered her elegance, and now she owns it. In fact, she credits the jewelry incident with giving her much of her courage. While on the campaign trail to become a judge, she met Walter Mondale. He congratulated all of the male candidates, wishing them luck, but when he got to her he stopped. "Why are you running for judge?" he asked.

"Because I look fabulous in black!"

Judge Moss knows herself, her worth, and her elegance. She developed it over time. You have to do the same. Define your own elegance. Choose it, then own it. That may mean a perfectly tailored suit or basketball shoes. It may mean yoga pants or a cocktail dress. Behind the uniform, only you can know every way in which you will choose elegance. But to truly know, you have to question, and you have to objectively and honestly consider what you discover.

Finding yourself is a process of discovery. My process started in law school. Law school is very competitive, and one of the competitions was to get the best class outline from students who had excelled in prior years. Some classmates would get the outlines, and then hide them from friends and even their boyfriends, girlfriends, and study groups. For me, all that hiding was not worth the potential for a better grade. That attitude carried into my practice, where I found that I was far more ruthless when defending others in my cases than when I was defending myself in my life's battles. I had to find a balance that was right for me.

Sometimes that's found in the uniform, and sometimes it's found in the way you do battle. But finding what is right for you is a process of discovery, one marked by questions, curiosity, and faith. I had to have faith in my elegance, in my choices and where they would bring me. I had to have faith that my discovery would lead me to ways I could win because of my elegance, and not in spite of it. You need to have faith as well. Trust in how far the right choices can take you.

PROVE IT

A warrior's uniform matters.[2] When you wear formal business attire, it makes you a better negotiator. Wearing white lab coats led one experimental group to commit half the number of mistakes, and this wardrobe choice also led to better performance when the wearer was told it was a doctor's coat rather than being told it was a painter's smock.[3] This may be due to a belief that doctors are smart. Finally, and perhaps most importantly, slightly deviating from one's "uniform" can be seen as positive because it shows you're strong-minded and courageous enough to risk the social cost of being different.[4] In another study, a man in a red bow tie at a black-tie event was seen as having higher status. This may be due to others' perception of competence, or to the way it made him feel. Choose what uniform makes you feel the most like you, and then wear it with pride.

SUMMARY OF THE CASE

1. Be true to your own personal elegance. Choose how you want to present yourself to the world, and be committed to a constant process of discovering what works best for you under different circumstances.

2. You don't need to conform to be elegant. Sometimes being authentic to your own personal truth is an integral part of the battle.

3. Know that the uniform does matter. Your presentation affects what others feel about you, but more importantly, it affects how you feel about yourself.

3

Be Curious

"The cure for boredom is curiosity.
There is no cure for curiosity."
DOROTHY PARKER

WHEN I WAS a little girl, my friends and I would go exploring. There was a construction site a few blocks from my house, and a bunch of us would ride our bikes there and look for treasures. I always wanted to find a fossil, something special to bring home and show off to my friends and family. I imagined I'd be in the paper, the third-grader who became a famous paleontologist. I dreamt of the fame and fortune my fossil would bring, though I now know there isn't a ton of money in fossils. My imagined story was a lovely one, but not lovely enough to make me stick with it. In time I realized that, for me, fossil fame was not worth the scraped knees and dirty fingernails. The discovery itself was hard work.

This truth became even clearer when I became a trial lawyer. Cases started with complaints, but then it was all discovery, all the time. There are typically two years between when a complaint is filed and when we go to trial. In those two years, we explore. We exchange written questions and answers with all of the other parties, then take depositions in which we trade questions and answers. Discovery is the drawn-out process of asking questions and getting answers. And each question opens the door to another fight over whether the question was proper, or whether the information sought will be relevant.

Like kids who have skinned knees and dirty fingernails from searching for treasure, the discovery process of a lawyer's fight can be dirty.

Sometimes I'd come home from a day of discovery empty handed, but when I was lucky, I found a treasure—an entry in the medical record that no one else had noted, or an unexpected admission at a deposition. Such treasures were far more likely to be uncovered when I'd approached the discovery process with real curiosity. As a lawyer, I found discovery to be a lot more fruitful if I approached it looking for *any* treasure, rather than specifically looking for a fossil—or the evidence I needed to win the case. The more curious I am, the better the discovery process goes.

One way to make sure I don't miss anything is to ask open-ended questions—those that require more than one word to answer—during discovery. The more I ask open-ended and curious questions during discovery, the more I learn. And this learning process starts at my first meeting with my client.

Experience brings a lot of gifts. I wasn't always this curious, or this good at asking open-ended questions. It used to be that, after going through the basic pleasantries, I'd ask my client specific questions about the case. I'd listen carefully to her replies, taking notes so that when she was done I could follow up on the details. Asking focused questions is one way to get information and perspective, and it's enough to win lots of trials. This style of questioning tends to work best when you're homing in on what you want—you already know the answer you are hoping for, and you know exactly how and where to dig for treasure.

But one phrase gives you space to learn more than you think you know. That phrase is "Tell me what you want me to know." I saw the power of this phrase in my work as an anchor at the Law & Crime network. We covered the sentencing hearing of Larry Nassar, the former USA Gymnastics and Michigan State University physician who pled guilty to multiple counts of first-degree criminal sexual misconduct. Over the course of the proceedings, Judge Rosemarie Aquilina heard testimony from over 150 girls and women who had been impacted by Nassar's behavior. Judge Aquilina didn't ask these girls, "What happened?" She didn't say, "Tell me everything you remember." She said, "Tell me what you want me to know." In that case, her open-ended approach worked magic. Every time she posed this request to a survivor, it seemed another survivor came forward. They seemed drawn to Judge Aquilina's curiosity and empathy.

If these eight words had this much power for these survivors, imagine what they could do for you. You could use this phrase in romantic relationships, in building better teams, and in growing closer to the children in your life.

I had the opportunity to ask Judge Aquilina about that request, and how she'd known to use those specific words. She told me the phrase came naturally, as she's always felt that in every case the story has to come from the witness. It's true that too often, in court and in life, our questions are an attempt to tell the story for the other person. We use our questions to project. "Were you mad?" instead of "How did that make you feel?" "Did you fight back?" rather than "What did you do?" There is a reason lawyers aren't allowed to ask leading questions: they're an attempt to give the answer. When questions try to give the answers they take the power from the person who owns them.

But with this one request, "Tell me what you want me to know," you learn a whole lot more. You might start out looking for fossils and find gold.

Now I use that request at almost every initial client meeting. Nothing else has allowed me as much insight into my clients' fears, their hopes for the case, and the information that they might not otherwise share. That request has allowed me to be victorious in cases I'd otherwise not have had the insight to win.

You can use the power of this phrase outside the courtroom as well. If you're arguing with someone you love, "Tell me what you want me to know" shows love. If you're arguing with someone you don't love, "Tell me what you want me to know" might provide a glimpse of potential resolution. When trying to find the way to a solution, "Tell me what you want me to know" shines light on a path you may not have otherwise seen.

The best explorers are curious, patient, and willing to be surprised. When it comes to discovery, whether in law or in life, we should strive for the same.

PROVE IT

Psychological studies show that people who ask more questions are better liked by their conversation partners.[5] So if you want connections, ask more questions. If you want to learn, ask more questions. Research that studied ten learning techniques found that practice testing with feedback provided some of the best results.[6] The evidence is clear—questions, and answers, make us smarter and more connected to one another.

SUMMARY OF THE CASE

1. Discovery is where the good stuff happens. It might lead you to a resolution, or give you the tools you need to win.

2. Curiosity is the key to discovery. You might be looking for fossils, but always be open to finding gold.

3. "Tell me what you want me to know" is the kind of open-ended request that gets results.

4

Move to Create Progress— or to Create Fire

"The world is wide, and I will not waste my life in friction when it could be turned into momentum."
FRANCES E. WILLARD

YOU HAVE TO know what you want in order to create it. Going after what you want requires motion, but motion only gets you where you want to go if you're heading in the right direction. And not all motion creates progress—if you are moving in the wrong direction, you lose ground. If you're moving against something, an idea or an opponent, you create friction. Friction can slow you down, but it can also start a fire. There are times when fire is what you want. It may be that you're ready to burn some bridges, and sometimes you need fire to light the way. But make a conscious choice as to whether you're trying to progress or trying to cause friction.

In lawsuits, motions are a written request for a judge to make a decision about a limited part of the case. Lawyers file motions to get things moving. Too often, in the law, things get stuck. Part of being a trial attorney is fighting, but since we aren't allowed to kill each other, we often come to an impasse. Then we have to file motions, go before a judge and play out a ridiculous version of tattle-tale that leaves us feeling less like capable adults and more like belligerent children.

Motion court can be a new attorney's dream or nightmare. It is where we go to present legal arguments before a judge in support of the written motions we've filed. Often, motion court is the first opportunity a new lawyer has to speak in court. But these rookie lawyers soon find out that the judges want them to find a compromise, not fight to win. My friend from law school found motion court especially frustrating. She would walk into the courtroom ready for battle, unwilling and unable to see the other side. She was there to create fire, not progress, and she burned down many an opposing attorney's argument. One day her adversary approached her when she came in the room, hoping to reach an agreement. She came at him with guns blazing until he finally sighed, saying, "The one with the orange handle is the decaf. Try it."

My friend wanted to create fire, and was not in the mood for progress. Motion can serve both masters, but not at the same time. You need to choose what you want motion to do for you. Do you want to make sparks fly, create a fire, and burn down the old ways? Then fighting may be the answer, and you can move in that direction. But if you want to move forward together, with a common goal for a common good, you need to find another way to make progress. And that means you need to undertake a different kind of motion.

I like to move forward, and save the sparks for when I'm ready to create an inferno. While I've chosen a job that is all about fighting, I avoid it when I can. As a lawyer, I pick my battles. Most of the time they're at trial rather than in boardrooms or in depositions, and most of the time I choose well enough that when I do have to go to trial, I win. As a defense attorney, I don't get to pick my cases. But I can choose when to file motions, when to fight them, and when to save the fire for the actual trial before the jury.

In life, picking my battles is harder. Here, too, I prefer progress over fire. There have been times when I've bitten my tongue to keep things moving. Choosing elegance often means ceding a battle or two.

You choose your battles, and you choose how to fight them. You have to ask yourself how much each battle matters to you and where you want it to lead. If you want to win, prove the point, slay the enemy—that is the time for fire, and fighting with no holds barred. But if you want progress, then forward motion—without friction—is your best bet. Choose your motion, and then go all in. So the next time you're in an argument with your partner over which TV show to watch, consider your goal. If you really want *The Bachelor* and he really wants *Ozark*, prepare for fire. But if you want a relationship based on compromise, choose progress and watch *Ozark*. Or better yet, watch *Game of Thrones*. Everyone seems to agree on that one . . .

In many battles, your biggest competition is yourself. Your ego may be looking for friction when progress will serve you much better. You've got to know who you are fighting in order to win. Fighting yourself is wasted energy—you always lose. You and your ego will enjoy the victory much more when you've combined forces to beat the enemy.

PROVE IT

Warriors have to choose between moving for progress or moving for fire. Choosing progress is not a sign of weakness. There are many health benefits to letting go of friction and opting for progress. For example, letting go of resentment can improve sleep.[7] And that extra sleep will help you when you do have to forgo progress and fight fire with fire.

SUMMARY OF THE CASE

1. Movement can create progress or friction. Both have their place. It's up to you to decide what you want, and where you want the movement to take you. Then get moving.

2. Know your opponent and decide how you want to use your energy. You have to know who you're fighting in order to win.

3. Many times when you think you have to fight, you're wrong. You're more likely to see a compromise when you start to move. That change in perspective could change everything.

5

Decide Whether to Get Dirty

"When they go low, we go high."
MICHELLE OBAMA

I WAS A RECENT law school grad, and my classmate's father, Mr. P, was on trial. Being "on trial" doesn't mean he was the defendant, but rather that he was the lawyer representing the defendant. In Philadelphia, lawyers use the phrase "on trial" to describe when we are in a trial. In other parts of the country, they say "in trial." Either way, it's the time for battle. I stopped in to his courtroom in City Hall to see if I could catch part of the case. I wanted to be the best trial lawyer I could be, and part of that meant observing as much as I could, to adopt pieces of each fighting style that worked for me. This man was an exceptional trial lawyer, and I wanted to see what I could learn.

When I slowly opened the courtroom door, the trial was in recess. The judge and jury weren't in the room, but the lawyers were. I went over to Mr. P and spoke to him briefly. He said they'd be starting up again shortly, though during the break he was trying to settle the case. This is what we do: we fight like warriors in front of the jury, then try to find a compromise when they step out of the room. In this negotiation, they were hundreds of thousands of dollars apart, which meant they were close. This was an amputation case, so the damages were high. Money has a different meaning in catastrophic cases, and hundreds of thousands of dollars is no longer a large chasm to cross. I ran to the bathroom so I could watch the battle when the jury returned, if the case hadn't been settled by then.

When I walked back into the courtroom, Mr. P was laughing as the opposing attorney, a middle-aged married man, walked away. He pulled me over to him and said, "He thought you worked for me, and said he'd take fifty thousand dollars off the demand for a night with you."

I didn't know what to say. I was young, and both men were established and well respected. I suspected I was going to be surrounded by other men saying similar things for much of my career, and behind them would be well-meaning men like Mr. P, uncomfortably laughing about it. Most trial attorneys are men. That meant that I didn't have many examples of how to handle the comment or the laughter. But how I handled both now would set the bar for how I handled them in the future.

I had options. I could raise my voice, tell both men I was offended, and demand that they never speak to me or about me that way ever again. But that didn't suit my definition of elegance. Making these men, who grew up in a generation where this behavior was accepted, feel abashed and embarrassed on their first strike wasn't my personal style, and yelling was not my answer. This was twenty years ago, long before #MeToo. I didn't feel that yelling would serve me or my clients—if these men were uncomfortable talking to me, trusting me, I might lose out on being included in conversations that I needed to hear. Trial lawyers tend to have many cases together over the years. I was bound to meet these men in other depositions and other trials.

I could ignore the comment completely, but that didn't work for the warrior in me. I thought about myself but also about the other women who had graduated from law school with me. None of us should have to worry about having our bodies bartered as part of settlement negotiations when we were trying to win our cases. Silence was not my answer either.

I waited until Mr. P looked up at me, wondering why I hadn't responded. I smiled slightly, maintained eye contact, and said, "I don't think that's funny. It's inappropriate. And it's gross." Then I waited, heart racing with adrenaline and fear. Would he laugh at me, or call the other attorney over to join the joke? He looked down at his papers, abashed. "You're right, and I'm sorry."

Since then, I've handled similar situations in different ways, depending on the circumstance, the battle I was fighting, and how strong I felt that day. I've ignored similar slights too many times. I've gotten dirty, swearing at an offender in a tirade born of frustration and exhaustion. But that day, as a young woman unsure of her place in the world and in that courtroom, I didn't stay silent (I was a warrior, after all) and I didn't freak out (elegant, too). I stated my case, and it felt right. You have to decide what feels right for you. First, though, you need to recognize outrage when you feel it. For many years, we laughed in order not to be laughed at. And now, the pendulum has swung. We're offended and we're not afraid to show it.

You choose how to express your elegance, and you choose how to express your outrage. For me that day, quiet confidence marked by a strong tone and steady eye contact worked. Both men remained my friends, and neither has ever spoken to me that way again. I was proud of how I'd expressed my outrage. And I've carried on that approach to my next battles.

Choose how you want to be and how you want to express your outrage, but do it consciously. If you decide to get dirty, then get dirty. Make it a conscious decision, and make sure that you aren't feeding the very behavior you abhor. As George Bernard Shaw said, "I learned long ago never to wrestle with a pig. You both get dirty and the pig likes it."

PROVE IT

Anger can help you win. Studies show that increasing anger levels before negotiation may lead to getting the other side to concede to participants' demands. For example, a study by Maya Tamir and Yochanan Bigman revealed that anger will often do what you expect it to do.[8] If you expect your anger to work for you, it may. Faith in your anger may make it more effective.

SUMMARY OF THE CASE

1. You will be outraged. Choose how to respond, and make that decision a conscious one. Choosing takes presence, mindfulness, and practice. You can find all three within yourself.

2. Getting dirty often makes things worse. You may be feeding the flames of your opponent's fire. Be aware of the strength of anger and use it wisely.

3. Don't immediately stoop to your opponent's level. When you do have to get dirty, bring all of your skills to bear on the fight. But remember that the hardest loss to recover from is the one where you lose the battle and your elegance.

6

Choose Your Army; Start with Your Mentors

"We need to stop telling [women], 'Get a mentor and you will excel.' Instead we need to tell them, 'Excel and you will get a mentor.'"

SHERYL SANDBERG

EVERY WARRIOR NEEDS a mentor to teach her the rules of engagement. For me, that was John. He was my boss, my uncle, and my guide. Every young lawyer, if she is lucky, has the opportunity to carry a lead attorney's bag. That means she goes with him to trial, watches what he does in the war room and in the courtroom, and learns. I learned more from watching John than I did in all of law school.

John spent years as a Drug Enforcement Administration (DEA) agent before he became a trial attorney, and he approached every trial like a sting operation. We didn't eat (except for Peanut M&M's) and we didn't sleep. While I didn't adopt that aspect of his practice, much of what he taught has become part of me and my practice. He was kind but tough, always a gentleman, and approached cross-examination like it was a battle. He rarely left the opponent standing.

After many months of sitting silently beside John while he brought together the work we'd done in the war room to wage battle in the courtroom, I was eager to step into battle myself. I was also afraid. It's one thing to prepare the weapons; it's another thing entirely to pick them up and use them in front of a room full of people, including and especially the client who is depending on you to win.

In this case, we represented two surgeons—an older, experienced attending surgeon and a young doctor who had assisted in the surgery. The young doctor was a fellow, done with her primary training but still working on honing her skills. The claim in the case was that the attending surgeon had left the room and allowed the young surgeon to do the surgery solo. I knew this was false. I'd spent sleepless nights in the war room, lining up all of the records from the hospital on the day of the surgery to establish that the timing worked. The attending was efficient and skilled, and he was in the room for this patient's operation. He'd done what he told the patient he'd do, and he'd done it well. We should win this case, and that heightened the pressure.

The patient's case is presented first, and John had cross-examined the expert against our doctors with the precision of the surgeons he'd represented for so long. He'd cross-examined the patient himself, gently and precisely. Now we were in our part of the case, and he'd done the direct examination of the attending physician, allowing the doctor to connect with the jury almost as if John wasn't there at all. It was time for the fellow to testify. John called her to the stand, and as she got settled John turned to me and said, "You do it."

What? I wasn't prepared, didn't have a single question written down, and hadn't worn my lucky suit. But the judge was waiting, the fellow was waiting, the jury was waiting, and

John was waiting. I stood, and I did my first direct examination. It was awkward and had no flow. It wasn't my best work, but it was enough. We won that case. And I learned what it is to have, and be, a mentor. A good mentor knows when to show you what to do, and when to let you do it. And a good mentor is there to back you up and slay any of the beasts you might leave standing.

You need to choose your mentor well, and keep choosing until the day you leave the battlefield. John is my forever mentor, the man I look to for guidance in the courtroom and beyond. But I've had an army of mentors since. You will have as many mentors as you choose to have, and they don't have to come from your specific battlefield. In fact, some of the best training can come from outside your area of expertise. If you're a mom who works inside the home, you might learn a lot from a CEO. If you're an artist, you might learn a lot from a retired nurse. Some of my best mentors have been doctors, midwives, mothers, and salespeople.

Remember, too, that every mentee is also a mentor. I've served as a mentor to many young lawyers. Some have approached me, in the courtroom or in the classroom, and asked me to be their mentor. Others have been assigned to me as part of the process of working at my firm. I've worked to be as good a mentor to them as John was to me. When you've received the training, you have an obligation to pass it on. But I've learned as much from these young mentees as they have learned from me. They've taught me enthusiasm, independence, and how to keep up with the technology that sometimes seems to be passing me by. A warrior never stops learning, and the lessons from my mentees have helped me continue to find victory at battle.

You get to choose your army. Choose your mentors and your mentees with an awareness that each one brings some individual strength that your army needs in order to win.

PROVE IT

Studies show that having multiple mentors provides stronger career satisfaction and success.[9] It follows that mentors from different fields can widen your knowledge base and your network. In addition, serving as a mentor results in greater job satisfaction and more commitment to your organization. And when you serve as a role model, your performance may even improve.[10]

SUMMARY OF THE CASE

1. Choose your mentors well, and let them teach you in word and in action. Part of being a mentee means recognizing that you're the student.

2. If you are the mentor, you too are a student. Be willing to allow your mentee to teach you what she has to offer.

3. Look outside your arena for mentors. The best lessons might be from those with experience you can translate to your field.

7

Be Quick to Laugh, Even During Battle

"There is little success where there is little laughter."

ANDREW CARNEGIE

THERE'S ALWAYS A reason to laugh. Find yours, and you'll find that the battles become easier. Laughing does not make you less likely to win. I used to think every trial had to be serious, and it's true that your clients and the jurors don't want to see you yukking it up in the courtroom. However, finding the laughter in the midst of a trial is good for your physical health, your mental health, and your chances of success.

Early in my career, I had a case in which I couldn't help but laugh. The patient had undergone spine surgery, and while he was objectively in better shape than before the surgery, he wasn't feeling as well as he'd hoped, and he was angry. In fact, it seemed he leaned towards anger in most situations. He found a lawyer to take his case, but he was the driving force.

This man attended every deposition and motion, and he made them interesting, even funny.

The first time I laughed out loud in a deposition was in his case. He came to the surgeon's deposition, and sat next to his lawyer just as my client sat next to John. I was there to learn, to provide John with documents, and to keep quiet. But I also had the opportunity to observe the patient when John and the doctor were busy dealing with the questions. First, I saw him shaking his fist at the doctor during the deposition, with a menacing look on his face. I got the giggles. Fortunately, I was able to control them for a while. I looked away, but when he continued to shake his fist, I kicked John and motioned for him to look. The look of utter confusion on John's face almost broke me. Then I noticed the patient was ripping up little pieces of paper, making them into tiny balls. I watched as he lined them up, and then put one in his mouth. He couldn't be doing what I thought he was doing! But he was. He proceeded to launch the spitball at the doctor. And I lost it. John lost it in a different way—he was enraged.

John stopped the deposition, but I couldn't stop my laughter. We all laughed, in shock and disbelief in the doctor's office after the deposition. We laughed even harder when the attorney dropped the case. It's tough to have a client who might launch spitballs at the jury.

It's good to laugh, even during times of trial. You can laugh and still be serious, and you can laugh and still be victorious. Being elegant doesn't have to mean being boring.

There are times when life seems nothing but trials. I had a period when I tried six cases in a row, and I didn't have much reason to laugh. Each case was different, with separate clients and unique medical issues. I had to compartmentalize them, remembering the issues of each and bringing them to the forefront when it came time to try each one. But I had to make room for laughter or else I wouldn't have survived. And I mean that. Laughter is that important. Learn to laugh in the midst of battle; and it will sustain you when you feel like you will never find reason to laugh again.

Laughter is a habit—the more you laugh, the more you'll find things to make you laugh. It's a way of being grateful, of praising what you have so that the universe brings you more. When you focus on the hard part of battles, that's all you see. When you widen the lens to let laughter in, you'll see so many more reasons to laugh. Challenge yourself to find a reason to laugh every day. Even better, keep a laughter journal and at the end of the day write down three things that made you laugh. The things you focus on grow, so focus on laughter and watch the joy grow.

PROVE IT

The health benefits of laughter are well established. Laughter stimulates organs, relieves stress, and soothes tension.[11] But laughter also helps us learn. Research shows it reduces anxiety, boosts participation, and increases motivation.[12]

SUMMARY OF THE CASE

---

1. You might think there is no place for laughter on the battle-field. You'd be wrong. The more you laugh, the more you increase motivation and decrease anxiety. When you are relaxed and focused it can only help the battle.

2. Laughter is a habit—you build it by doing it. Find a reason to laugh, and you'll find more reasons to laugh.

3. Laughter is a way to give thanks. The hardest and most important battles are for things to be grateful for, and laughter is an ideal way to express that gratitude.

8

Collect Your Yeses

"I think a lot of people dream. And while they are busy dreaming, the really happy people, the really successful people, the really interesting, engaged, powerful people, are busy doing."

SHONDA RHIMES, FROM *YEAR OF YES*

HE SAID, "NO." First he said it with his body. When I walked into the room, weighed down with the big black binders that contained every detail of his case, I could see him shake his head and cross his arms. I was ready for him, though. I'd expected the no.

This doctor was an older man, from Venezuela. He'd been represented for the entire case thus far by one of the partners at my law firm, an older man. However, that man was sick and unable to try the case. The trial was quickly approaching, and the other partners had asked me to step in. I'd tried a handful of cases by then. I'd done well. I had also spent the entire weekend learning every aspect of this doctor's case. I knew I could try it. But he didn't know it, not by a long shot.

"Where's John O'Brien?" he asked. John was my boss, and his name was on the law firm's door. He was also my uncle, but we had different last names and I was glad for that. I didn't want people to think this young woman was able to try cases so soon in her career due to nepotism. In fact, I went out of my way *not* to take advantage of John or our relationship. And there was no way I was telling this doctor I was his niece.

"John is meeting with another client this morning," I said. "I'd like to try this case with you. I know you don't know me, so why don't we spend some time going over your medical records. When we're done, you can decide what you want to do."

He reluctantly agreed to meet with me, but still insisted he wanted a partner to try the case. For the next five hours I showed him why such a young woman had been allowed to try cases. I knew every inch of every document in every huge black binder. I had strategies planned for every potential issue. I had studied the medicine, and I knew as much about cardiac catheterizations as any layperson could know. I had earned a yes from this doctor. But that didn't mean I would get it.

Getting yeses is hard. I'd been fortunate, though. Deb Lorber gave me my first yes—she let me try my first case. After that, the yeses came more quickly and more easily. But there were still nos. Often, they came from doctors like this one, who didn't think any young female could stand up to an older male in the courtroom. With this doctor, I once again had to earn my yes. I had to prepare more than anyone else would, and answer more questions than anyone else could.

And I did. At the end of our meeting, he said yes. And we won our case. Since then, I've collected many first yeses. Sarah Marx, a producer at Fox News Channel, gave me my first yes to be on TV. It was for Shepard Smith's show, and he said yes as well. Dan Abrams gave me my first yes and hired me to anchor on his new Law & Crime network. My first key-note, my first consulting client, my first coaching client, my first book—I keep collecting first yeses. When you stop asking for yeses, you stop living.

In order to get your first yes, you have to be willing to ask. Asking takes chutzpah and the knowledge that you can do what you're asking to do and can face the consequences if you fall short. All of those things are at your disposal, and they all come from preparation. Prepare for the ask, and prepare for the yes. Know what you'll do when you get it. Prepare for the good results and prepare for the bad. If you focus on earning and collecting yeses, you'll find they come more easily. And as you grow, you'll become the person who gives others their first yes. Be sure to share them. Yeses are like all of the best things in life—including love, laughter, and success. The more you give, the more you get.

PROVE IT

According to Linda Babcock and Sara Laschever, authors of *Women Don't Ask*, women . . . don't ask. They found that men initiate negotiations about four times more often than women, and 2.5 times more women feel "a great deal of apprehension" about negotiating. You can't collect yeses if you are unwilling to ask for them. More women, and men, need to be willing to seek the yes. The good news is that recent studies show that younger women are more willing to go for the yes.[13]

SUMMARY OF THE CASE

1. Ask for your first yes, and keep asking. When you ask before you're ready, the answer gets you ready for the next ask. The goal is to collect the yeses.

2. You have to be willing to earn your first yes. Some people have their first yes handed to them; most don't. Be ready to show anyone who is looking that yes is their best answer.

3. Pay it forward. Sooner or later, you'll be in the position to give what you've received. Don't hold on so tight. When you share the yeses, they tend to grow.

9

Rest

"Have regular hours for work and play;
make each day both useful and pleasant,
and prove that you understand the
worth of time by employing it well."
LOUISA MAY ALCOTT

DURING THAT PERIOD when I had six trials in a row, I almost had a breakdown. I was in the car, heading into *Good Day Philadelphia* to do a television spot, and I started crying. I was exhausted, with two trials behind me and four more ahead of me, and I couldn't see the light at the end of the tunnel. I sat in my car and fought the tears (I didn't want to ruin my makeup) but could feel myself losing my breath. My chest was heaving. I needed to take a rest or winning would be impossible.

When I was a very young lawyer, John had a heart attack in the courtroom. John and I were on trial, and it was the perfect storm. The patient was catastrophically injured, paralyzed from the waist down after a surgery in which our client was the anesthesiologist. Our client was a good man, and we liked him. Over the course of the case, he had become our friend. The attorney for the patient was also someone we considered a friend. That was why I was so surprised at how ruthless he was once trial began. I shouldn't have been. Trial lawyers are meant to be advocates, and that often means leaving friendship at the door of the courtroom. The trial had been a bloodbath, with the attorneys on both sides fighting with all they had to bring victory for their clients. In the process, I was sure that some friendships, and some people, would never be the same. I didn't know how right I was.

After two and a half weeks of trial, the jury was sent to deliberate late in the afternoon. John and I went home to sleep, though you never sleep when the jury is out. The next morning, I walked into an eerily quiet courtroom. Silence in court is like silence in church—it echoes. John was alone in the courtroom, sitting on the bench with tears in his eyes. I was happy to see him sitting, and resting, after so many weeks of pacing and movement. I wasn't happy to see the tears.

"What's the matter?"

"Chest pains."

One look at him and I knew this was a tragedy waiting to happen.

"Go to the hospital!"

"No."

John is stubborn, and nothing I said could change his mind. I was starting to cry, and ran to the hallway to see if there was someone who would help, but I was unsure of what help would look like. Pete Divon, the judge's assistant, was rounding the corner. I begged him to make John go to the hospital. Somehow he did, and in fact he personally got him there. They left and I stood alone, in a silent courtroom. For a moment everything was still, but I knew I couldn't rest. Soon the client, the attorney, the judge, and the jury would arrive. When they did, the jury came back with a verdict. We were done, but I still couldn't rest. I ran to the hospital to see how John was doing.

John had a heart attack, but he survived. With time, and with rest, he got better. And I began to see that we all need rest in order to get better.

During our trials, John and I didn't stop. Three days or three weeks, whatever time it took to fight the war was time spent with little sleep, food, or rest. We didn't pause to rest.

Now I know to rest, even during times of trial. I'm friends with an accomplished patient's attorney. He relaxes by meditating every night, even when he is on trial. He knows that in order to have the stamina to fight, you need to rest, so he makes the time and space to do so.

I used to think I wasn't trying if I wasn't exhausted. I had to be spent. Now I know that effort doesn't have to be all in, and that taking the time for rest gives me the time and space to find things that might just lead to a win.

I know that sometimes things seem too much to handle. They're too hard, too long, too much. But before you quit, try taking a rest. What that looks like depends on where you are in your life. Sometimes it's a deep breath in your car before you find a smile to show on television. Other times it is a meditation (or a drink!), during the silence of the evening, in the midst of a trial. Whatever rest is for you, take it.

Put down this book and take five deep breaths, eyes closed, mind focused on where the breath is going. Breathe in through your nose, and out through your mouth. Breathe in whatever it is you need to face the next moment as the person you've chosen to be. Breathe out anything that doesn't support that endeavor.

You will discover that in the rest, you will find the time, energy, and motivation to keep going.

PROVE IT

There are a host of studies that support the premise that an incubation period leads to better problem-solving and more creativity.[14] During the time that we believe we are resting, other forces appear to be at work. Rest often leads to results.

SUMMARY OF THE CASE

1. When you stop to rest, you avoid quitting altogether. In trials, taking that moment to breathe might make the difference between victory and defeat.

2. If you use your time at rest to consciously breathe, and focus on breathing in your nose, that breath is feeding your creativity and your ability to solve problems.

3. Life is meant to be lived in cycles. There is a time to sow and a time to reap. Put in the work, and then take the rest that you need.

10

Nurture Your Team

*"You can do what I cannot do. I can do what
you cannot do. Together we can do great things."*
MOTHER TERESA

WHEN WE NEEDED to prepare for trials, John and I
would go to the war room. Armed with binders full of
records, highlighters, tabs, Peanut M&M's, and Diet
Cokes, we'd shut ourselves in and build our battle plan. It was
also where we built our team, and we couldn't have won as
much as we did without both the plan and the team behind
it. During the trial, John was the one standing, vulnerable, in
front of the jury. But it was what we created in the war room,
the tools the team gave him to attack and defend, that allowed
him to slay. John knew the power of strong teams from his
years as a DEA agent. He couldn't go undercover without a
team supporting and protecting him. He approached each
case the same way. That meant sleepless nights and too many
cigarettes and Diet Cokes, but also loyalty, camaraderie, connections, and trust.

After days spent sweating in the war room, starting trial actually felt like sweet relief. For me, anyway. It was harder for John because he was the one who had to actually stand before the jury and argue our case. On the mornings of openings, I'd round the corner to the courtroom to find him pacing the halls, legal pad in hand, working on his opening. I'd keep walking, giant blowups of the exhibits in my arms and butterflies in my belly. Part of being a good team member was knowing when he needed time to pace. At the start of my career, my most important jobs were to carry the exhibits and know when to keep quiet. I had to use my intuition to read what he needed so that the team could win. I had to know when to speak and when to listen.

You have your team, whether it's your family trying to get everyone out the door to school or your sales team trying to meet quota. And in order for your team to succeed, you have to make connections. Everyone must speak, and everyone must listen. From hospitals to huge companies like Google, from households to grocery stores, communication makes teams work. It creates a feeling of trust and psychological safety, which is the secret to creating a winning team.

The research on psychological safety has established that it consists of intuition and proportionate speaking—that means every member of a team should be speaking for about the same amount of time as everyone else. So at home, both parents get equal time, as do the children. At work, the boss speaks as often as the employee. I'd also add proportionate listening to this list. How safe can anyone feel if they're speaking but no one is hearing a word? If you are asking questions, listening to answers, and tuning in to the emotions behind both, everyone is speaking and listening, and your team will be closer to victory.

Ask more questions and make them personal. You might think you should avoid personal questions at work, but you'd be wrong (within reason). The more personal questions you ask, the more connected you become to your team. Curiosity creates connections, and connections are the cornerstone of the best teams. Build your teams, and then nurture them. No warrior can win without an army, and you must cherish the army that allows for your victory.

John retired years ago. I miss him every day, but when I look back on those days in the war room, I miss him even more. Things have changed, and now I work remotely, at home, most of the time. That means I prep for my trials alone, communicating with my team primarily via phone or email. It's convenient and it allows me to do my consulting, keynote speaking, and television work. It allows me to work at 3 a.m. if I want. But it's also lonely, and it makes trial prep much lonelier. We worked hard in that war room, pacing and arguing and outlining examinations. But we also laughed a lot. The laughter is what made the trials unforgettable, and our teamwork and trust in each other allowed for the laughter. Sometimes it's the team itself that makes the game worth playing.

PROVE IT

Psychological safety is the key to teams that work and learn well.[15] This is true in hospitals and in tech hubs like Google.[16] Be sure to take advantage of opportunities to share this experience, because it makes things easier. In studies, when people had a friend by their side and were asked to climb a hill, they perceived the hill as less steep than those who were about to climb it alone.[17] When you have an ally, any war is easier to fight.

SUMMARY OF THE CASE

1. You don't have to fight alone. Recognize when it takes an army to win, and choose yours well.

2. Teams need to feel safe with one another in order to offer suggestions and engage in creative thinking. In turn, those suggestions and that creative thinking make you feel more psychologically safe and more resilient. It's a victorious circle.

3. Building a team is a start, but nurturing that team is the key to consistent victory.

11

Know When to Settle

"Compromise is the best and cheapest lawyer."
ROBERT LOUIS STEVENSON

BELIEVE IT OR NOT, settling is often the best option. Sometimes you settle for more than you expected, and sometimes you have to be willing to settle for less. If you're not willing to settle, you're going to risk losing when you could find a compromise that would allow everyone to win.

Settling was very hard for me when I was a young lawyer. I didn't become a trial lawyer to settle—I wanted to win. At some point in every case I've had, opposing counsel has made a demand to settle. I used to dread that moment, because it was often the beginning of the end of the war. Suddenly the battlefield had changed, and I had to join forces with my opponent to find a solution. I always strived for compassion and collegiality, but going from conflict to collaboration in the blink of an eye was enough to give me whiplash. While I always knew that settlement was an option, I often doubted it would ever become a reality.

It was even harder for my clients. I represent doctors who have dedicated their lives to helping people. They've sacrificed their personal needs and time with their families, and invested loads of money into healing others. And then a patient files a complaint, which the doctor reads as "You made a mistake, and you hurt me." Doctors take this more personally than you might think. For many, it's truly one of the worst experiences they'll go through. Some doctors I've represented can't continue practicing medicine, because either they no longer trust their patients or they no longer trust themselves. Most doctors find that when they're sued, they're not inclined to settle. As their counselor, I have to find a way to help them explore what it is they really want. At first, many of them want a lawyer who yells. I have to show them that the one who wins isn't always the one who yells loudest. Rain grows more flowers than thunder does, and even the rain can hurt if it falls too hard and fast. Being open to a settlement is sometimes the soft rain that allows for growth. When the doctors stop wanting to see a fight, then I can explore what it is they really want.

If they want peace of mind, or affirmation, or justice, they won't always find it in the courtroom. While I trust the system, jurors are human beings who want to believe doctors can help them. They don't want to believe that doctors can't fix everything, and the intricacies of the medical issues are often overcome by strong emotion and the lizard brain, the survival instincts calling out "Don't let that happen to me!" Justice may be blind, but it's also human. Settlements are often the best, and safest, way to end a lawsuit and get on with a life.

You might want to consider settlement, too. Ask yourself what it is that you really want. Do you want to be right and win, or do you want to be happy and settle? It takes presence of mind to remember to ask this question, and to listen for the answer. Taking time to rest is a big part of that mindfulness.

Ask your inner voice the right questions, and it will tell you when you're ready to put down your sword. You'll know when you have to fight and when you only *think* you do.

What do I want? Where will I find it? And what does victory look like? These are the questions that lead to victory, and when you recognize that victory doesn't have to be bloody, you will find yourself winning much more often, and much more easily. War has casualties, and it should always be a last resort.

PROVE IT

Studies show that people who sue do better financially when they make a deal.[18] Knowing this often makes my clients *more* likely to want to fight. They often don't want the people who sued them to do better financially. But every advantage comes with a trade-off, and winning a case doesn't come without losses. Researchers have established that the psychological damage of lawsuits can be greater than the damage of the underlying event.[19] I've seen cases almost kill people. I know the value of settling for more than that.

SUMMARY OF THE CASE

1. Every offer to settle, whether in the courtroom, the boardroom, or the bedroom, is an opportunity. Don't let your ego make you miss it.

2. You have to know what you want in order to get it. And often what you want is not victory on the battlefield, but rather in your heart. Choose what a win really means to you.

3. Sometimes it is only in settling for less that you're able to gain much more.

12

Pick People Well

"Every day brings new choices."
MARTHA BECK

EFORE THERE WERE e-readers, I looked for the books. When we choose jurors for trials, over fifty people stream into the courtroom and take their seats for voir dire. This is when lawyers get to learn a little bit about the jurors, ask them some questions, and then pick our people. It's the only time lawyers get to ask questions of jurors, which is how we choose our jury. Most of my cases have been tried in Philadelphia, and there the jury selection process is short. We have four to eight hours to try to measure a person's heart and mind, and decide whether or not he can be fair to our side. It's our only chance to listen to the jurors, before they have to spend days, weeks, or more listening to us. There is never enough time, and every bit of information helps. The book a juror brought with her to jury selection answered some of my questions, so I could use our limited time together to ask others. While it's true that you can't judge a book by its cover, I often did judge a juror by her book. If she was reading John Grisham, she'd want to serve and may think she knew the law as well as the lawyers. If she was reading a school book, she might be distracted during the trial. Books could tell me a lot. E-readers and smartphones have stolen that tool.

There are television shows dedicated to choosing a jury, and people whose careers are based upon helping lawyers choose their juries. Choosing a jury takes skill, but more than that, it takes presence. When the jury panel walks into the room, I put down my phone and my pen, and I observe closely. I try to use as many of my senses as would be socially acceptable (taste and touch are not). I look at the jurors, watching their body language when they interact with one another in the main room, as well as when they come back to the room where the lawyers sit. I listen to their conversations with one another as they wait. If they smell like cigarette smoke, I know that they may bond outside with the other prospective juror who smells like cigarette smoke. Small details become important.

You are choosing people every day. In the past week you may have chosen a date, a doctor, a babysitter, or a barista. You base these choices on convenience, chemistry, your own biases, but also on what your senses tell you. Sight, smell, hearing, and even touch are the cornerstones of good choices. Don't let them go to waste. When it comes time to choose, put down the phone. Ask the kids to read quietly for a bit. Be completely present while you interact with the potential choice. You'll then be able to read the body language, micro-expressions, and tone that allow you to make the best choices.

Next, ask questions. Asking questions gets its own chapter a little later, but for now, rest assured that it's the best way to get the information you need in order to choose. When possible, work ahead of time to determine what questions are most important to your decision. Ask those questions first, then really listen to the answers. When you do, you'll find another question in the answer. Follow up, and ask it. The one who asks the most questions wins.

You also have to know when to stop asking, and when to trust the answers. More information helps, until it doesn't. At some point, you must stop collecting information and make a choice. One of the advantages of picking a jury is that we *have* to pick. The people who work in City Hall want to go home, so I can't stay there all night second-guessing my decision. I have to do my best, use the information I've acquired by asking questions and observing, and then make a decision. You can and should do the same. Gather your observations, then make a call. Go on the date. Hire the assistant. The great thing about real life is that if you don't like what you've chosen, you can make changes.

In the courtroom, we get what we get, and we can't get upset (unless something pretty major occurs). Fortunately for you, outside the courtroom you have the ability and the right to change your mind. So make your decision, secure in the knowledge that most of the time you can decide again and decide better. Practice picking the best people for the job at hand.

PROVE IT

Read body language. Most body language experts will tell you that if someone laughs with you, they feel close to you. When someone is smiling, check around their eyes for crow's-feet, as that is a sign the smile is real.[20] (This is harder in the age of Botox.) Crossed arms often mean the listener doesn't agree. All of this is helpful, but you must remember that all body language depends on context. If someone always has his arms crossed, it's not a sign of anything. Spending more time with a person allows you to read his body language more and more effectively. And when it comes to emotion, tone of voice can actually tell you more than all of your other senses combined.[21] We will talk more about tone in the next chapter, but for now, know that closing your eyes can often allow you to see more than you might imagine.

SUMMARY OF THE CASE

1. Picking people takes presence. (Say that five times fast!) The more you observe, with all of your senses, the better you will be at making a decision.

2. Body language, micro-expressions, and tone of voice provide real information that can help you make your choices. Become familiar with them, and use them to your benefit.

3. Choose. When you agonize over a decision, you're wasting time and energy. Make a choice; if it doesn't work, make another. Act. If that doesn't work, react. Don't let your ego make a decision—even a bad one—a bigger deal than it is.

13

Use Your Voice

*"It only takes one voice, at the right pitch,
to start an avalanche."*

DIANNA HARDY

IT WAS A VERY complicated medical case, involving an alleged delay in diagnosing cancer. The patient had sued three doctors, and the jury had to decide whether the defendant doctors had missed the diagnosis, but also whether an earlier diagnosis would have mattered. Therefore, this jury had to understand complicated testimony about the growth of cancer. I'll be honest—I didn't totally understand it myself. One of the experts started drawing a picture involving pi, and all I could think of was key lime or pumpkin. Our jury was made of up normal people, some of whom didn't have more than a high school education. They were bored and tired. That meant some of them fell asleep during this complicated testimony. More than once, the court officer had to come by and wake them up with a nudge and a glass of water. But every time I spoke, they all paid attention. They woke up, looked at me, and listened, if only for a moment. But a moment is all you need. Moments like these add up to wins.

They were listening, because my voice was different. The patient himself was a middle-aged man, his attorney a middle-aged man. The first doctor was a middle-aged man, his attorney a middle-aged man. The second doctor? Middle-aged man, his attorney a middle-aged man. My client, too, was a middle-aged man, and then there was me. Every time I spoke, the jury heard something different, which made a difference. At the end of the case, we were the only ones who won. Was that because of my voice? I don't know, but I know it didn't hurt that the jury paid attention when I spoke.

Your differences are your secret weapon. No one else can say what you have to say, and no one can say it the way you will. The world needs your perspective, your questions, and even your objections. Have faith in the value of differences. Have faith in your own voice and use it.

Sometimes your voice will shake. Expressing your differences is scary in a world where conformity is the norm. But a shaking voice still shares its message. Just because your voice is soft and shaky doesn't mean your message isn't loud and clear. It might be that the shakiness itself, your vulnerability, is the difference that will allow you to win. Beat your doubts, be yourself, and become the victor.

PROVE IT

Behavioral scientists have researched the power differences can have in "positive deviance." They define positive deviance as "intentional behaviors that depart from the norms of a referent group in honorable ways."[22] Whistleblowing is one example, but so are creativity and imagination. When men's voices are the ones we most commonly hear, a woman's voice is a positive deviation. An introvert speaking up, shaky voice and all, is the type of deviation that benefits us all.

SUMMARY OF THE CASE

1. Everyone has something to say, and if she doesn't use her singular voice to say it, that thing may never be said.

2. Our differences are often our strengths, and we can maximize the value of our differences when we know them well and use them to our benefit.

3. A shaky voice still wins trials. Even if your voice isn't steady, shake and stammer your way to victory.

14

Open to Impress

"A good first impression can work wonders."
J.K. ROWLING

OTHER LAWYERS' OPENINGS seem endless to me, while mine seem to take less time than the minutes it takes to apply my lipstick and put on my earrings. That may be my ego, but when I'm on trial, I wait for the other lawyers with impatience bordering on frustration. My leg shakes, and I go cold. I'm like a racehorse ready to leave the stable. The longer they talk, the more I work myself into a lather. If jurors are watching my body language rather than the lawyer who is closing, I'm sure I'm giving them plenty to read.

During the last case I tried, there were multiple defendants. This meant that by the time it was my turn to open, the judge had the jurors take a bathroom break right before I could go. It was torture. I was eager to use my skills to tell my client's side of the story. But lawsuits are orderly, and the person suing always goes first. Their attorney opens first, they put on their evidence first, they close first, *and* they get to do rebuttal. They have the burden of proof, so it's only fair they go first. They even get to sit closer to the jury. I see sitting farther away from the jury as a gift—too close and the jury might see me sweat—but letting the other side go first can be painful.

Openings are the first time the jury hears anything substantive about the case. Think of your first kiss, your first car, the first time your baby smiled—firsts are important. People remember the first thing they hear and see. Lawyers have to capitalize on that opportunity. You can do the same, any time you have the opportunity for a first. The first time you do anything—meet someone, make an entrance, get in a fight—you set the tone for all of the other times that will follow. Take advantage of the first time by making sure it is memorable, and that the memory is a good one.

Openings are meant to be an outline of the case. We lawyers are not supposed to offer argument during openings. We are simply to put forward an outline of what we believe the evidence will prove. Too many lawyers make this opening far too long. They get into minor details, losing the theme of the case. Juries don't yet know the details, so they need the theme; without it, they're lost. Most lawyers have the Curse of Knowledge, and it can hurt their case every step of the way, but the Curse is deadliest during openings.

The Curse of Knowledge is best understood by playing "Name That Tune." During my keynotes, that's often exactly what I do. I hum a song in front of a huge audience, and it's usually painful. I ask them to guess the song. If I'm lucky, it doesn't take too long. Sometimes they never get it, which makes my point but also makes me edgy. I know the song, and I have a hard time imagining what it is like not to know it. I have the Curse of Knowledge. That's what happens to lawyers during their openings. They know the case so well that they can't imagine not knowing it. They use words the jury doesn't understand. They get into medical issues the jury has not encountered. This is how you lose a jury, and sometimes the case.

About five years ago, I started doing legal analysis for Fox News, CNN, and other news outlets. It has made me much better at overcoming the Curse of Knowledge. When you have three minutes to make your point, you learn to be clear in a hurry. You don't get to have the Curse of Knowledge, or else the viewer will change the channel. You learn to speak in words that people understand. When you're used to having only three minutes, you can find it much easier to make your opening in fifteen minutes and not the hour or more that some judges will allow.

When you're about to make a first impression, think about the Curse of Knowledge. You know something this person doesn't. How does that knowledge impact the connection between you? Find ways to overcome the Curse, or use it to your benefit. If you pretend it doesn't exist, you hurt your chances at a win. You can overcome the Curse by asking questions. The more you ask, the more you know and the better you explain. Questions help you know your audience and what they understand. That new knowledge allows you to hone your message, and then repeat it.

In the courtroom and the boardroom, it is imperative that we overcommunicate. That's what it takes to drive a message home. A bad lawyer repeats herself. A good lawyer repeats her message, through different witnesses, and in different ways. Show them, tell them, ask them, answer them, then repeat. If you've had the chance to ask questions, you're able to really know your audience. If you don't, it could be fatal to your argument.

During my last trial, when one of the experts was called to explain the rate of cancer growth to the jury, it was as if he was humming the tune of a song they didn't know. It was our job to teach them a new song. You can do the same. Communicate with pictures, sounds, motions, and common sense. Start well. A first impression, when it is clear and concise, can set the stage for a win.

PROVE IT

There is a psychological principle that first encounters with new facts have a greater impact on later thought.[23] This is why openings are so important, in law and in life. We can use the power of openings by knowing when we are making a first impression, and making it a good one. The power of openings and new experiences may be why even if your first wasn't your best, you still remember it. Think of your first car, your first boyfriend, or your first kiss. It may not have been the best, but you will never forget it. If we work to make that first impression the best impression we can, we can harness the power of firsts.

A good way to ensure that memory actually means something is by overcoming the Curse of Knowledge. Once we know something, we have a bias against a "less informed perspective."[24] If we can overcome this Curse of Knowledge from the very beginning, meeting our partner or boss or jury member where they're at, we will make a great first impression.

SUMMARY OF THE CASE

1. There's only one first time. Don't squander your chance to communicate who you are in this moment.

2. Often we lead with our knowledge, but if we know too much, we may be unable to understand that others don't have that knowledge. The Curse of Knowledge is indeed a curse. Empathy is the key to overcoming this curse, and we gain empathy by asking questions.

3. You may need to overcommunicate to get your point across. This doesn't mean saying the same thing over and over, but rather saying the same thing in different ways. If you can say it seven time in seven ways, you'll probably make your point.

15

Strike with Questions

"In this universe we are given two gifts: the ability to love and the ability to ask questions. Which are, at the same time, the fires that warm us and the fires that scorch us."

MARY OLIVER

M Y FAVORITE PART of trial is when I get to cross-examine the other side's experts. This is my chance to attack by asking questions, and when it works it is heaven. Questions are the most valuable weapon in your arsenal. You can use them to fulfill your curiosity, or to slay your opponent. The choice is yours.

I had the privilege of representing one of the most well-known thyroid surgeons in the world. Not only had he operated on thousands of patients, saving lives as often as he brushed his teeth, but he'd also written extensively on the complications that could happen during the surgery he performed most often. He did what he could to ensure that other surgeons would have the benefit of his experience and avoid that complication as often as possible. It wasn't possible to avoid it completely, and in our case the patient had suffered that complication. The expert against us said the complication had occurred because my client had made a mistake. We said it was an unfortunate complication, but one that cannot be avoided completely.

My client had written hundreds of articles on this complication. The expert hadn't written one. But the question was, had the expert read them? Because I had done so, I knew them, and I was ready to go toe to toe with him.

I had the articles in a huge pile, color coded and tabbed. When the expert approached the stand, I put them on my table and saw that he looked at them nervously. He didn't know what was in that pile, but he sensed it was dangerous. I waited impatiently for opposing counsel's direct examination to conclude, eager to do battle. Finally, it was my turn to question. One by one, I went through my doctor's articles that showed this complication happened in the best of hands and under the best of circumstances. One by one, the expert admitted he hadn't read them. I continued, and the jury leaned forward, rapt. When I'd gotten halfway through my pile, they started to shake their heads in disgust at this expert who hadn't taken the time to read the defendant doctor's articles. Twenty more articles in, and again the expert said, "No, I didn't think it was necessary to read it."

"You didn't think it was necessary to read a peer-reviewed article, written by the doctor you've come from Alabama to Philadelphia to criticize, on the exact topic you are supposed to be explaining to this jury?"

At this point he was tired, and no longer fighting.

"No."

"How much did you say you were getting paid for your testimony?"

The jury laughed. Then they cringed when he informed them that he was being paid thousands of dollars. For any lawyers reading, I'm aware that opposing counsel could have objected. I took my chances and chose to ask the question, even if it went unanswered. The question itself made my point.

You can use questions to win. First, try using them to build connections. When you ask questions, you build camaraderie, and you can help people see things from other perspectives. Asking questions helps you trade perspectives. If that doesn't work, and battle is inevitable, use questions to tear apart the opponent's argument. Phrase your question like a sniper would take aim—ask quickly and with purpose. Questions are your weapon with the biggest impact. They're like a Swiss Army knife. They can be used to attack, but also to impress, to learn, and to explore. When it comes time for you to use your questions, first you must know how you want to use them. Start with the end in mind. When you do, you'll find that good questions get you closer to that end more than almost anything else can.

PROVE IT

Questions can be used to earn trust[25] and they also increase the chances that others will like you.[26] Studies also show that in speed dating, the people who asked the most questions got the most second dates.[27] There are entire classes and books on how lawyers can use questions to win. You can use questions to succeed, too.

SUMMARY OF THE CASE

1. You can use questions to do just about anything. Choose what you want to accomplish, and then focus on *how* to use your questions to achieve that goal.

2. You think you have to fight, but perhaps all you have to do is ask.

3. When you have to attack with questions, don't be afraid—be prepared.

16

Remember
the Power of How

"Your video needs to match your audio."
ROBIN SHARMA

I DON'T BLUSH. I used to yearn to blush, like the heroines in the novels I read. Pink cheeks were pretty, and I wanted to be pretty. Then I became a trial lawyer, and I found out that pretty didn't matter much. It was much more important to be cool, especially under pressure, and if you couldn't be cool, you could at least look cool. Cool people don't blush.

John was cool. I remember one client who was tough to prepare, difficult to get focused, and emotional when challenged. He cared about his case, a lot, and he'd work and prep with us, a lot. Then he'd go home and worry, a lot. When he'd call John at 11:30 p.m., while we were hard at work in the war room, my job was to answer the phone and give him the kindness that he needed. The night before his testimony, as you might expect, he was especially on edge. I knew we'd done all we could to prepare him, but I also knew he was nervous. When we hung up, I was nervous—not because I didn't feel confident in our case or our client, but because a client's nerves can look like a lot of things before a jury.

With this client, nerves looked like arrogance. The doctor spoke quickly, avoiding eye contact with the jury. He kept his hands on his lap and picked at his nails, looking down as he testified. When he did look up it was to look at John, not at the jury. John carried on, doing his best to show the jury what we saw in this doctor. We knew our doctor was kind, funny, and smart. John asked him about his education, and why he'd chosen oncology as a specialty. John was trying to put him at ease before he got into the crux of the case, a conversation during which the patient claimed the doctor hadn't given her key information about the medication he'd recommended. That medication had side effects, and those side effects had led her to lose her leg. If the jury believed the doctor, we'd win the case. If they believed the patient, we'd lose.

John asked the question, tall and proud, with quiet confidence. "Did you tell her about the risks of this medication?"

"No."

Thank God the jury wasn't looking at me. I know that I visibly flinched. I jerked my head, tensed my body, and grimaced in frustration. John did not.

"You didn't discuss the risks of this medication with Mrs. M?" John asked, still quiet and serene.

His serenity finally sparked something in the doctor, who realized his mistake and corrected it.

"It was more than a discussion. It was a conversation, one that went on over many visits and many telephone calls…"

With that, the doctor's body language changed. He began to connect with the jury, leaning forward and using his hands. He smiled as he described the positive interactions he'd had with his patient. He dropped his shoulders and slowed his speech. With each change, the jury responded. They uncrossed their arms, turned their heads towards him, some leaning forward to mirror him.

I've never had a case, before or since, in which body language was so clearly on display. I've studied many books on body language. I've learned how much of a story hands and feet can tell. I know that I'm better when I use my hands as part of my communication, and when I speak slowly, making eye contact. I try not to let the podium stand between me and the jury. But the best lesson I've ever learned about body language came from that case and that examination, because John communicated so much with his question.

How you ask questions matters. How you do anything matters. The how might be just as important as the what. Body language, tone, stance, and micro-expressions make a difference. If John had stammered, moved to his notes, or showed any surprise at the doctor's answer, things might have ended differently. The client might have become more agitated and nervous, feeding off John's energy. The jury might have trusted both of them less, put off by the intangibles that are anything but inconsequential.

What you do matters, but *how* you do it matters just as much. The two have to match to have the most impact. You can work on the Power of How in your own life. It starts by being aware, and for a while that may mean pretending that you're always being watched. At times when I'm facing something challenging, whether it be a trial in the courtroom or in life, I pretend I'm on stage. Doing so helps me control my how. I'm less likely to lose my temper, less likely to swear, less likely to let my emotions get the best of me. I also work to tune in to the energy of the interaction. This works better if I meditate regularly, not just during the trial, so I'm able to tune into energies more easily. If you get very good at working the how, you will ultimately be working the energies in the room. I've seen very good lawyers, preachers, speakers, and counselors do this. But before you can control the energy in the room, you have to be able to control your own energy. All of this takes presence, which leads to using body language, tone, and awareness. Use the Power of How—to accomplish your goal—to win.

PROVE IT

The *how* of communication is important. Studies show that when the nonverbal communication (tone, body language, expression) doesn't match the verbal (the words being used), you're better off trusting the nonverbal to relay the speaker's attitude.[28] When the audio and video don't match, trust the video. That means it is important to be aware of how others are communicating with you, and how you are communicating with others.

Meditation might make you better at reading body language. One study showed that meditators were even more skilled at making mind–body connections than dancers were.[29]

If you're wondering how to master the Power of How, meditation is a good place to start to be aware of what your video is telling people.

SUMMARY OF THE CASE

1. *How* you do things communicates just as loudly as *what* you do. Sometimes the how can even drown out the what. Choose your how with intention.

2. You can be the master of your how, especially when it comes to body language. Choose how you want to be and

then put in the work. Imagine you're on stage. If you want to do things with elegance, think elegance. If you prefer brazen, think brazen.

3. Practicing your how takes mindfulness, and meditation helps. Remember the how, over and over again.

17

Be as Good as Your Word

"A promise made must be a promise kept."
ARISTOTLE

I F THEY DON'T believe me, I can't win. It's that simple. When I stand up to address the jury, I have to connect with credibility, because that is the basis of our relationship. The same is true for you—if you don't have credibility, you don't have much.

Sometimes, when the trial is over and the verdict is in, the judge asks the lawyers to stay and talk to the jury. This is much more fun when you've won than when you've lost, but either way I think it's a good idea. It allows jurors to get a better sense of the legal process and to ask the questions they aren't allowed to ask at trial. (Though some states do allow jurors' questions, the states where I've practiced do not.) Talking with the jury also allows the lawyers to see what they did right, and what they can fix for the next trial. I've had many such discussions and learned a lot about what I can do better. I've learned that jurors are human, and that the fact that I'm a woman elicits different questions. After one particularly long trial, the jurors had questions like "Why do you always wear your hair up?" and "Why do you always wear pantsuits?" They don't often ask such questions of men. While I'm happy to answer (both are due to convenience and ability to move quickly and unencumbered), I don't learn much from those questions. Other times the jurors have given me gold, and the biggest nugget was this: credibility is everything. Time and time again, jurors have said they believe me, even when they don't believe my clients or my witnesses. They trust what I say, and that is the greatest compliment I could receive.

When I stand to give my opening, I know that everything I'm about to say can be proven with evidence. If I tell the jury what I expect a witness to say, I have to know that witness will say it. For example, sometimes I'm able to tell the jury that the expert for the patient, whom they have to believe for the patient to win, will say X, Y, and Z. I'm able to do so because I've spent weeks reviewing that expert's past testimony, where they've said X, Y, and Z. Now, in our case, that expert will either have to say it or contradict himself. Either way, it's a win, which bolsters my credibility. If I tell them about a medical record, I have the record. If I tell them about a medical issue, I've researched the issue. I have the literature.

This is crucial, because at the beginning of the case the jury doesn't know me. They don't have to trust me. I have to build that trust, and it starts at the opening. Then, throughout the case, they see that they can believe what I tell them. I've said an expert will agree that a wound that won't heal is a sign of a circulation issue. When I cross him, the expert may not agree, but that works for me, too—I have an old deposition where he has said it. And when I show this deposition to the jury, they see I've told them the truth and the expert hasn't. If you want to win, you need to build that kind of trust.

Step by step, slowly and painstakingly, the trial continues this way. I say it, and I PROVE IT. I tell them, then I show them. I've built my credibility, one piece of evidence at a time, and now I can rest my case on what I've built.

Everyone needs credibility to succeed. You need credibility with your kids, with your partner, and with your colleagues. Credibility needs to be built, and to build it you need to be willing to put in considerable time and effort. Say it, then PROVE IT, and win. This takes patience, because the process can be slow. Credibility is not built with words. The proof is in the action. "I'll pick you up at 8." And you're there. "I'll do this project well." And you do. "I will be faithful to you, to our relationship, to our ideals." And you are. Once credibility is built, it is the strongest foundation for any relationship. When it is shot, the relationship might die.

When we build credibility at trial, we do it with evidence. You need evidence, too. You can build credibility with evidence of honesty, patience, time, and hard work. None of this comes fast or easy. It means you also have to be honest about what you can't or won't do. If you tend to be late, say so. People would rather a late person than a liar. If the project is too much, too hard, or you don't have the resources, say so. That kind of honesty allows teams to work around the potential hurdles, and that kind of vulnerability captures hearts. If you don't agree with your partner's ideals, discuss them. It's the only way to come to a meeting of the minds, and hearts. Not doing the job, not being on time, not being faithful to ideals won't necessarily cause you to lose, but loss of credibility will definitely affect your ability to win.

PROVE IT

PricewaterhouseCoopers' 2016 Global CEO Survey showed that 50 percent of CEOs considered lack of trust to be a major threat to their organization. In his book *The Trust Factor: The Science of Creating High-Performance Companies*, Paul J. Zak shares research showing that people at high-trust companies report 74 percent less stress, 106 percent more energy at work, and 50 percent higher productivity. It is clear that no matter what you do, you do it better when there are trusting relationships. Credibility builds that trust.[30]

SUMMARY OF THE CASE

1. Credibility is the key to winning over hearts and minds, and that's in turn the key to winning our trials and our battles.

2. Be careful what you say. If you can't PROVE IT, you may lose credibility, and then you've lost everything. This isn't hyperbole. If you don't trust your partner, your clients, or your children, the relationship will not thrive. And if the jury doesn't trust me, I've lost ... everything.

3. Proof is more often in the action than the words. When you make a promise, keep it. When you set an expectation, meet it.

18

Prove It—with Evidence

*"Take nothing on its looks; take everything
on evidence. There's no better rule."*

CHARLES DICKENS

"**W**HAT'S YOUR EVIDENCE?"
This is my go-to question. When my niece tells me
another child at school is being a jerk, I ask. When my
friend says she thinks her job is in jeopardy, I ask. When I'm
convinced I'll never make it as an author, I ask. Evidence is
important. It's where you find your proof. It is the basis of
everything else. Evidence is what you use to meet expectations,
and you can't exceed expectations unless you've met them first.
Juries expect me to prove my case with evidence. Your custom-
ers, your clients, your colleagues, and your families expect you
to prove yourself with evidence as well.

In court, there are two types of evidence. There's direct
evidence—what you actually see and hear to prove the case. For
example, when a patient has a scar on her leg, it is direct evidence of damages. She has proof that she was hurt. A contract

is direct evidence of some type of agreement. But there's also circumstantial evidence—the evidence you don't personally see or hear but that you can infer. An example is that same scar, used to prove that a surgery happened. We didn't see the surgery (a video would be direct evidence), but this scar can help us to infer that a surgery occurred. The judge usually describes circumstantial evidence to juries by telling the story of going to bed at night.

"If, when I am going to bed, I look out the window and it's snowing, that is direct evidence that it is snowing. However, if I don't see it snowing, but the next day I wake up and there is snow on the ground, that is circumstantial evidence that it snowed last night. I didn't see it happen, but I can infer that it did."

As you might expect, in my cases, most of the evidence is circumstantial. Unless we have a video of the surgery, it's very hard to find direct evidence of any alleged mistakes during the surgery. But circumstantial evidence is evidence enough. It can be used to prove my case just as well as direct evidence. You prove your case with evidence, and circumstantial evidence is enough to win.

In life outside the courtroom, we have both direct and circumstantial evidence as well. Take my niece. If she says, "That kid is mean," the direct evidence might be that kid pushing another kid. The circumstantial evidence would be the scratch on the victim's arm, or the tears in his eyes. Circumstantial evidence might be more common, but it is also subtle. You have to pay attention to notice it. But once you start paying attention, you'll find the evidence is clear, and things become easier to prove.

Start to pay attention and you'll see evidence everywhere. Now you can use it to make your case. You want a raise—find evidence of your value. You want your child to have extra help in math—find evidence of his need. You can also use circumstantial evidence to win. Body language is circumstantial evidence. So is tone of voice. Deep sighs, passive-aggressive behavior, unresponded-to emails—all circumstantial evidence. When we start paying attention, we find the building blocks of victory. At work, your job is to prove your value; do it with evidence. At home, your job is to prove to others that you value them; do it with evidence.

It also helps to check yourself with evidence. Nothing is true until you PROVE IT. When you start thinking, "That guy is a jerk," force yourself to find the evidence. When you start thinking, "I'll never be able to do it," see if there's evidence to support your claim; often, you'll find there is no evidence. A thought without evidence to support it isn't a fact; it's just a thought, and thoughts can be changed.

Even when you do think you've got evidence to support your thought, you may need to explore further. Evidence can often be used to support either side of an argument. Here's an example. I do a lot of consulting work with call centers. Recently, I worked with a call center for a medical office. These men and women spend all day, every day, talking to sick patients. It's a hard job. The patients are often in pain, impatient, even angry. The call center employees have to maintain their cool and, in the best cases, their empathy. They have to listen for not just the words but their tone and meaning. It's exhausting, and often thankless, work. This group certainly felt that way. In our discussions, time and time again I'd hear, "The doctors don't care about what we do" and "They don't understand."

I asked what I always ask: "Where's your evidence?" They had none for the first thought, "The doctors don't care about what we do." "PROVE IT," I challenged. They couldn't. However, their proof for the second thought, "They don't understand," was clear. The doctors didn't know the process by which calls were handled. They didn't know the level of emotion on the calls, or the frustration that patients would share. And the evidence for that thought also gave us understanding into the first thought. Maybe the call center agents would feel that doctors cared more if doctors took the time to learn what they did every day.

We had to PROVE IT. We talked to the doctors about the call center employees' roles. The call center agents themselves told the doctors, during relaxed happy hours we held for them to spend time together. Some doctors even came over to the call center to watch what the agents did. The result was that the doctors understood what the agents did. And, perhaps more importantly, the agents had evidence that the doctors cared about what they did. Everyone won.

You can use evidence to prove, or disprove, your thoughts. Whether you're talking to yourself or others, you'll find that evidence is the quickest route to success. Amanda, my amazing editor, has a note on the inside of her front door that says, "You also learned to walk." What better evidence that you can do things that seem hard at first!

PROVE IT

In court, jurors routinely undervalue circumstantial evidence,[31] possibly because of the "beyond a reasonable doubt" standard. In life, there's no such standard and we routinely depend on circumstantial evidence to prove ourselves and our beliefs.

SUMMARY OF THE CASE

1. Thoughts aren't always true. To test them, consider the evidence you have to support your belief.

2. Most evidence is circumstantial. It's found in tone, body language, and feelings. To get the best possible evidence, we have to tune in to the circumstances around them. What is unsaid often means more than that what is said.

3. You have to prove yourself *and* PROVE IT to yourself. Evidence is required to accomplish both goals.

19

Show It 'til You Grow It

"Don't fake it 'til you make it. Show it 'til you grow it."
HEATHER HANSEN

I'D NEVER ASK a witness to fake anything. Jurors do not like fake. I once represented the most wonderful dermatologist. He was brilliant, kind, and cranky. Really, really cranky. Even his voice mail message was cranky. The voice mail would come on and he would just yell his name, "SIMON MILLERSON!" and then the beep. For our first three meetings, I was convinced he hated me. He wasn't mean, but he wasn't friendly. He was just gruff.

If I'd asked Dr. Millerson to be cuddly, sweet, or friendly on the stand, the jury would have hated him. It never would have worked. And he probably would have yelled at me for asking. Instead, I worked on questioning him in ways that would show how much he cared, and in ways that would allow him to show it. I couldn't ask him to "fake it 'til you make it," because he was never going to "make" sweet. But I could work to show his attention to detail, using the phone calls he made to the patient before and after his procedure, to be sure the patient was comfortable (body and soul), as evidence. When I asked questions that showed how much Dr. Millerson cared, he settled into the questioning and the jurors' vision of his caring grew.

On cross-examination, Dr. Millerson was beyond cranky. I knew he would be, and it definitely worried me. He yelled at the patient's attorney, shook his head in frustration. But the jury told me afterwards that they loved him. They'd seen his caring, and they shared his frustration. He'd shown his caring, that caring had grown as he spoke, and in turn he grew on the jurors.

If someone tells you to fake it 'til you make it, run. Faking it doesn't work, and it doesn't feel good. If you lose yourself by faking it, you can never win. But you can find that thing inside of you that will help you win. It may be your smarts, your caring, your sense of humor, or your empathy. Find that thing inside of you that makes you feel most yourself, and most confident, and show it. As you show it, it will grow. Show it 'til you grow it, and you end up with everything you need.

Start by listing the qualities you are most proud of, those in which you have the most confidence. Then take that list and determine where those qualities can be used in the situation at hand. Your sense of humor could be used to charm, to put people at ease, or to add some light to a dark situation. Once you decide how you can best use it, it's time to show it. The more you show that sense of humor, the more people laugh. The more people laugh, the more confident you feel and the more it grows. Find out what your inner "it" is, then show it, then grow it. The first step is the most important, and it is the step that "fake it 'til you make it" overlooks. Fake it at your peril.

You can show it 'til you grow it at work, at home, with clients, and with friends. Take that spark inside of you, that only you know exists, and start to show it. That spark will get the oxygen of attention, love, and respect, and it will grow. You'll win, but more important, you'll win without losing yourself.

PROVE IT

Amy Cuddy is well known for her research on body language and faking it 'til you make it.[32] In her book *Presence*, Amy argues that when we act confident, we become confident. She encourages readers to do a "power pose" before a big interview, and allow that pose to give us confidence. I agree with the posing, but not with the faking. Amy's research supports the idea that when you show the confidence you have inside, that confidence can't help but expand.[33]

SUMMARY OF THE CASE

1. You simply can't fake it 'til you make it. Real results take real input. Find what you have that's real, and start there.

2. When you show something that's real, you will get what you need to make it grow. When you show the real you, even if it's hard to do, the real you can't help but eventually prosper.

3. Show it 'til you grow it. The resulting wins will amaze you.

20

Learn to Object

"No one can hurt me without my permission."
MAHATMA GANDHI

YOU HAVE TO learn to object. Sooner or later, you're going to have to stand up, use your voice, and set your boundaries. Even for a trial lawyer, it's not always easy. I learned to object in the courtroom. You might think that after three years of law school, all while clerking at my current law firm, I'd have learned to object before I got to trial. But it's one thing for people to teach you about objections; it's another thing entirely to make them.

Objections are the way a lawyer lets a judge know that something is wrong. We use objections to put the judge on notice that we believe the other side has violated the rules. The judge then has to decide on the objection. *Sustained* means she agrees that the rules have been broken and the lawyer making the objection wins. *Overruled* means that the objecting lawyer loses and no rules have been broken. Objections are a lawyer's way of saying "This isn't okay."

My first real objection was, fittingly, during my first real trial. It was a short and simple case, as a lawyer's first trial should be. My client had performed a hernia repair on the patient. The patient's claim was that my doctor had made a mistake and that the scar from the surgery was too big and he hadn't known it would be so large. We had to prove to the jury that my doctor had a conversation with the patient about the incision. I'd given my opening, and done my direct and cross-examination with ease. But any objections I'd had to make were easy, half-hearted ones, objections I knew would be sustained. They weren't risky. Now the case was over, and we were in closings. The patient's lawyer gave his closing while I sat, legs jiggling in eager anticipation for my chance to speak to the jury.

As I listened, the patient's lawyer said something I knew was wrong. It was legally improper. I should object, but I was afraid. If I were wrong, and the judge yelled at me, the last thing the jury would remember would be the judge telling me I was wrong. But I knew in my head, heart, and gut that he was wrong. Everything inside me was begging me to object. When lawyers object, we stand to be heard. So I stood, but then I sat. Stood again, sat again. Half up, half down. Anyone watching would think I was playing some deranged game of Whac-A-Lawyer. I glanced at the judge, and he gave me the eye that said, "Do it already." I took every bit of confidence I'd built throughout the case and I stood. "OBJECTION, YOUR HONOR!"

That was over twenty years ago. I won the objection, and the case, but I still had a lot of work to do. I had to learn to object without getting someone else's permission. I had to give myself permission to stand up, use my voice, and set my boundaries.

And so do you. There are things in your life that you'd like to change. Every life has its trials, and if you want to win, there are times you have to object.

In the courtroom, I've developed a three-step process to making objections. You can use it in your life's trials as well. First, stand up. Action precedes motivation. We've talked about showing it 'til you grow it. Well, the best way to show it is to move. Nothing happens until you move, so try moving and the rest might follow. Second, use your voice. I gave this aspect of facing and winning trials its own chapter (chapter 13) because it's that important. Your voice makes you different, and your differences help you win. Finally, set your boundaries. In the courtroom, the judge decides objections. But in life, you are the judge of your boundaries and whether they've been violated. No one else knows the line and when it can be crossed. When you draw that line with purpose, defending it becomes that much easier. You'll object with grace and confidence.

PROVE IT

When you're ready to object, stand up! Your body is the manifestation of your personal power. If you feel powerful, your body shows it.[34] Next, use your voice and capitalize on your differences. Finally, set your boundaries. Boundaries are an important part of establishing your personal identity and your self-esteem.[35]

SUMMARY OF THE CASE

1. For some of us, learning to object is one of the hardest lessons of all. Those who are scared of it need to learn it the most. Don't underestimate the power of a well-placed objection.

2. Learning to object requires action and the ability to rely on what makes you different. Stand up and use your voice, and you're on your way.

3. No one can set your boundaries for you. When you've determined those boundaries and are comfortable with them, you'll find yourself much more comfortable defending them.

21

Overcome Objections

"We were scared, but our fear
was not as strong as our courage."

MALALA YOUSAFZAI

IT'S NOT ENOUGH to know how to object; sometimes, you're going to be on the receiving end of objections. You need to know how to overcome them. Luckily, you can do it with two words: "So what?"

I learned the power of those two words in a judge's chambers. I was about to start a huge trial involving a catastrophically injured young woman. She had a wheelchair and a breathing tube, and her arms and hands were rock hard, occasionally wracked with spasms. The demand in the case was ten figures, and we were trying to settle the case for much less.

The patient's attorney had been talking to the press about her condition for weeks leading up to the trial, and I finally had the opportunity to bring it to the judge's attention. He wasn't happy, and he told the attorneys on both sides not to talk to the press about the case, to avoid any potential for impact on the jury. When I turned on the TV that night, I saw opposing counsel on the news, talking to the anchor about her client's breathing tube and her wheelchair. I didn't sleep all night, incensed and eager to tattle on her.

The next morning I did, and was satisfied when the judge was even angrier than I was. He asked the patient's attorney to explain herself. The lawyer attempted to explain that she thought she could talk about the injuries, just not the case. No one was buying the argument, not even the attorney making it. Finally she sighed, looked at the judge, and said, "So what?"

I was in shock. I had never, would never, say "So what?" to a judge. The judge didn't seem to know what to do. He shuffled some papers and looked at us with a frustrated sigh. "We're going to have to ask the jury whether they saw that newscast. And I'm going to have to fine you." But the potential verdict in this case was millions of dollars, so the fine seemed more of a nuisance than a punishment. So what, indeed.

We all need a little more "So what?" in our lives. It is the greatest ally we have when we are trying to overcome objections. Because the objections that are most dangerous, the ones we have to worry most about, are our own. When I was a young attorney, my own objections stopped me far more than those of opposing attorneys ever have. I stopped myself before asking that evocative question, afraid of the objection. I stopped myself before using that creative exhibit, afraid of the objection. I was objecting, and ruling on my own objections, before my ideas ever got to see the light of day. My own objections were my biggest downfall. That changed when I started saying "So what?" What could happen, and how bad would those possibilities be?

The other attorney might object. So what? The judge might yell at me. So what? The jury might laugh, I might not know the answer, my client might be disappointed, I might be disappointed. So what? I asked myself that question, and really answered. "So what?" always had an answer, and the answer was never that bad.

This self-questioning carried on outside the courtroom as well. If I wrote a book, people might not read it. So what? If I said no to my boyfriend's request to go to the amusement park with him and his son so I could write instead, he might be frustrated. So what? If I pulled back on trials to focus on writing, speaking, and consulting, I might make a whole lot less money. So what? I found that the answer to each "So what?" wasn't fatal. Sometimes I'd decide to do the thing, and sometimes I wouldn't. So the objection would be denied or sustained.

When you're working to overcome objections, your own or others', your secret weapon is "So what?" But using that weapon gets a lot easier if you've prepared. For me, overcoming objections, in and out of the courtroom, is a never-ending cycle that always starts with preparation. You can't overcome an objection if you aren't prepared, because your answer to "So what?" will always be potential catastrophe. So you prepare, and then you may be the first voice to object. Your own objections are usually just holding you back from your dreams. Objection overruled!

PROVE IT

It takes confidence to overcome objections, and confidence is vital to success. In fact, finding your confidence can begin with the answer to a simple question: "So what?" It's especially important for women to embrace this question, as there are hosts of studies showing that women tend to have less confidence than men. *The Confidence Code*, by Katty Kay and Claire Shipman, discusses many of these studies. But the real problem may be that women have more confidence in the rules than men do. Tara Sophia Mohr believes that this confidence in following the rules holds women back more than their own lack of confidence.[36]

SUMMARY OF THE CASE

1. Objections aren't fatal, and the best way to overcome them is to ask yourself, "So what?" The answer is usually not as bad as you'd imagined.

2. Your own objections can be the hardest to overcome. Stand up to yourself, and really own the answer.

3. Confidence is everything. The more you overcome objections—especially your own—the more confident you become.

22

Stop Looking for Objections

*"When you change the way you look
at things, the things you look at change."*

WAYNE DYER

JUST LIKE LOOKING for trouble, if you go looking for objections, you'll find them. In the courtroom, they're everywhere: leading, hearsay, argumentative, irrelevant, outside the scope, prejudicial... the list goes on. Many young attorneys spend a lot of time looking for objections. You don't want to live that way.

I once had a deposition in which I had multiple co-defendants. The patient's attorney, Mr. B, was an old, established, and connected man, used to getting his way in almost every circumstance. The attorney who asks for the deposition questions the witness first, and here that attorney was young, inexperienced, and enthusiastic. She had her questions, and it was obvious that she'd overprepared. Her questions were good in substance, less so in style. She knew what she wanted, but was less clear in how to get there. Though she had definitely practiced her questions, Mr. B quickly showed her that practice did not always make perfect.

"What did he tell you?"

"Objection!"

"I'll rephrase. What did he say?"

"Objection!"

And with that, she moved on to another line of questions, and Mr. B preened with pleasure. The deposition continued that way for hours, and during those hours I wondered what Mr. B was actually getting. He got to flaunt his experience and his ability to control the young attorney. But he didn't get any information that might help his case, or see any of the warning signs or omens that could mean disaster for his case at trial. He was so busy looking for objections that he wasn't seeing or hearing the actual information that could be vital to his case.

Looking for objections might make you miss the win. When you're looking for objections, you're not seeing all there is to celebrate. You're not hearing the sounds of fear or love in the voices of those you care for, and you're certainly not living your fullest life. Looking for objections is a lot like looking for reasons to be offended. You'll always find them, but you'll miss a whole lot in the process.

When you're looking for objections, you're on the defense, and sometimes being defensive makes you paranoid, risk averse and, well, boring. I know this because that was me. Twenty years of defending medical malpractice cases has made me paranoid about what my own doctor might miss when seeing me as a patient. It's made me less likely to take the risk of putting something out in the world that others might object to, and when I do take that risk it's made me primed for battle with anyone who disagrees. Looking for objections makes it hard to be creative, spontaneous, and carefree. The only way to avoid objections is to be perfect, and perfection is not fun. It's not beautiful, sexy, joyful, or interesting.

When I first decided to start pursuing more creative ventures, I started objecting. It was outside my area of expertise. It was outside my comfort zone. It was uncomfortable. But I realized that I had to stop being my own lawyer. Because defending your art or your choices or your life is exhausting and unnecessary. There are reasons to object, in court and in life, but you don't have to look for them. You'll know them when you feel them, and when that happens your objections will come from the heart. They'll have gravitas.

So, find the balance between looking for objections and looking for a life. If you're afraid of missing an objection, you will miss so much more. You don't have to object to everything, and the things that you most need to object to will find you, for better or worse.

PROVE IT

The Baader-Meinhof principle shows that something you've just learned or been told about seems to pop up constantly.[37] It makes sense, then, that when law students are taught the bases of objections, they see objections everywhere. And sometimes when we realize we can object, we go overboard—our sensitivity overcomes our predominant sense. The evidence is clear—if you look for reasons to object, you'll find them. And if you look for reasons to celebrate, you'll find them, too.

SUMMARY OF THE CASE

1. Looking for objections is a good way to find them. You find what you seek.

2. Looking for objections might actually be a distraction, taking your attention away from the important facts that will be more likely to lead to victory than any objection ever could.

3. Don't be afraid you'll miss an objection. The important ones will make themselves known, loud and clear.

23

Be Your Own
Best Advocate

*"I always wondered why somebody doesn't do something
about that. Then I realized I was somebody."*

LILY TOMLIN

S HE WAS AN expert witness, but she was also a paid witness who refused to tell the truth, even if it was her
own. It was my job to catch her in lies. On this day, I did
my job well.

This expert claimed that my client, Dr. L, had failed to diag-
nose a rare skin disease. The patient came to Dr. L with a sore
on his finger that hadn't healed, and pain when he moved the
hand. Dr. L thought it might be infected, and the infection
might have traveled to the bone. He ordered an MRI to look
for osteomyelitis, a bone infection that can lead to amputation.
When that study came back clean, Dr. L referred the patient to
a vascular doctor, a specialist in circulation. Dr. L knew that a

non-healing sore and pain can be due to a circulation problem. I had to show the jury that Dr. L did everything right.

The expert who testified against Dr. L told the jury Dr. L did everything wrong. She said Dr. L should have immediately suspected this rare skin disease and done tests for that disease. The jury listened to her attentively, while I squirmed in frustration. I'd have my turn to advocate, but it couldn't come soon enough. First, the jury would have to listen to the lies.

Finally, it was my turn. I used questions to advocate for my client, to show my evidence, and to build my credibility. I also used my questions to go in for the kill. I'd read everything this expert had ever written about sores, fingers, and circulation. I'd reviewed every interview she'd ever given. Part of advocacy is being prepared, and I was. Another part is asking the right questions in the right way. I had to box her in.

"Do you agree that a non-healing sore can be a sign of a circulation problem?"

"Do you agree that the patient had a non-healing sore?"

"Do you agree that pain can be a sign of a circulation problem?"

"Do you agree that this patient had pain?"

"Do you agree that a vascular doctor is the best referral when you suspect a circulation problem?"

The expert should have answered yes to each of these questions. I knew this, not only because yes was the right answer, but also because she'd written or said that exact thing. I had read it in her articles and her depositions. It was black and white, but she wanted to go gray.

"Not in this case. In this case it was more deadly."

"Nope. He had a rare skin disease."

"Not here. Here, it was a problem that was growing by the minute."

"Pain from a rare and dangerous skin disease."

"Not in this case."

Lawyers are hired to be advocates. Experts in med mal cases are supposed to be hired to tell the truth about the medicine. While there's often more than one truth, this was ridiculous.

One by one, I took her own articles showing where she'd said essentially said yes to every question I'd asked, and showed them to the jury on a huge screen. One by one, she had to admit that this was an article she'd written to teach medical students and other doctors how to approach a non-healing sore. And with each admission, the jury leaned away from her and towards me. I'd proven my point, with patience, preparation, and practicality. We won that case.

I find it far harder to advocate for myself than for others. I can advocate for my clients, my family, my friends, and my employees. But when it comes time to fight for what is right for me, my voice shakes and my hands tremble. The best way I've found to advocate for myself effectively is to look to the same guidelines I use when I advocate in court. It comes down to the 3PS: patience, preparation, and perspective.

You've got to be patient. Since, as attorneys, we advocate with questions, we have to wait for the answers. You can do the same. If you ask questions and then listen, you get the answers you need to advocate for yourself and win. You've also got to be prepared. This can be harder outside the courtroom, as you don't always know when a trial is heading your way. When you know one is coming, get your facts and your questions ready. But when you don't, you can still know yourself. Prepare by knowing where you can bend and where you will break. Prepare for your weaknesses, and work to conquer them ahead of time, so they don't conquer you in battle. Finally, you need perspective. You have no authority with people you don't understand. When you work to understand your audience, you become a much stronger advocate.

PROVE IT

This is a hard one to prove, and that in itself is telling. While numerous studies show the benefit of learning to advocate for ourselves when we are young, they often focus on students with disabilities. But we all need these skills—when fighting for ourselves, and when consenting to others. Given that people are hiring patient advocates for medical situations, and teaching "no means no" on school campuses, advocating for ourselves is clearly an issue. We should look to trial lawyers for guidance. Trials are the place where advocacy skills have been on display for hundreds of years.

SUMMARY OF THE CASE

1. If you're willing to go to battle for others, you should be willing to go to battle for yourself.

2. Asking questions may be the strongest way to advocate to win.

3. An effective advocate follows the 3PS: patience, preparation, and perspective.

24

Don't Deny the Damages

*"The scar meant that I was
stronger than what had tried to hurt me."*

ANAÏS NIN

IT IS HARD to fight the damages. In my cases, the patient
has to prove duty, breach, causation, and damages. A doctor has a duty to his patient, a breach would be a mistake,
and that mistake has to have caused damages (in other words,
"no harm, no foul"). Often, I concede duty—a doctor has a
duty to his patient. Arguments about breach and causation are
where cases are won and lost. It's more challenging to win on
damages, because it's hard to argue that someone isn't hurting.
I learned that firsthand, outside the courtroom.

All I wanted was a fun summer weekend. I'd been dating my
boyfriend, Jon, for about nine months. We were at that point
in our relationship where we were just starting to have real
fights, the kind that make you wonder whether this is going to
work. The summer had been hard on us. I lived in Philadelphia,

where I was a partner in my law firm. I had a condo in Fitler Square, a share in a shorehouse in Avalon, and a life that I loved. Jon had a home in Connecticut, a job in New York City, and a son he adored. We had to make a lot of compromises, and compromise is hard—especially for a lawyer.

One of those compromises had been less time at my shorehouse. I missed my friends and the easy days of spikeball, cocktails, and dancing at the Princeton. I needed an Avalon weekend. So we made plans to spend the weekend in Avalon and go to all of my favorite spots, do all of my favorite things. But man plans, God laughs. On Friday night, Jon started feeling sick. His stomach was bothering him, and he said the beer tasted like it had turned. He rarely complained, and had an iron stomach, so this was unusual. That night, all night, he was up sick. This, too, was unusual. Jon was thirty-nine years old, in relatively good shape, and he hadn't been sick in our entire relationship, not one day. But he was making up for it now—dry heaving, with stomach pains that wrapped around to his back. I rubbed his back, pressing in hard to the place in his lower back that seemed to hurt the worst. I offered him Gas-X, which did no good. I asked whether we should go to the ER, but he refused. He said he'd be fine.

The next day, he was not fine, but he tried to be. He sent me to the beach, saying he'd try to make up for some lost sleep. After his nap, he rallied and came down to the beach to meet my friends, who had only heard of my new boyfriend. He chatted with them, and when a woman in a wheelchair needed her chair carried up from the beach, he and another man picked it up and gave her a lift. But he looked sick, and while he did come out that night, he couldn't eat or drink anything. Again, we were up all night with his stomach pains.

Defending doctors has given me health-care anxieties. I see the worst, so I look for the worst. I kept asking him if we should go to the ER, and he kept telling me it was a stomach bug. However, on Sunday morning I insisted he call his primary care doctor, and she thought it could be a kidney stone. She recommended we go to the hospital.

We debated whether to go to the local hospital or drive back to the apartment we shared in New York and go to the hospital there. Ultimately, we chose the latter. I drove, and Jon leaned his car seat back and chatted with me on the three-hour drive. Our exhaustion had us impatient, and when we pulled up to the hospital Jon said if we couldn't find parking, we'd just go home. We found parking. He said if there was a wait, we'd just go home. There wasn't a wait—in fact, the ER was eerily quiet. So we went in, they took a history, and we were put in a triage room with a curtain. They took Jon's blood and gave him some Milk of Magnesia. I pulled out some depositions to take advantage of the wait and prep for my next case.

Suddenly, the energy changed. A hand ripped the curtain open, and what seemed like hundreds of people hurried into our little space. They began taking off Jon's shirt, putting wires on his chest, and hooking him up to monitors.

"You've had a heart attack."

Time stopped.

"You've had a heart attack. We need to get you into the cath lab. The cardiologist is on his way. You've had a heart attack."

Jon turned to me and said, "Am I going to die?"

We'd always said that Jon has nine lives. He was born extremely premature, and the doctors weren't sure he'd survive. Then he took a hockey puck to the eye as a young boy, and had a bleed behind that eye that once again had him living in the hospital, this time for months. Later, as a young journalist, he'd been in a terrible car accident, breaking his back and his ankle. Years later, working in Iraq, the truck right in front of him was blown up by an IED. Jon was a survivor.

"No, you're not going to die. Look at all you've been through. You're like Superman. You're not going to die." But I had no idea.

As the ER team started to wheel Jon away, the cardiologist, Dr. Iyer, approached his bed. He looked me right in the eye and started asking questions. "Tell me what happened. What happened next?" I reviewed the events of our weekend with a shaky voice. He told me that he was going to take Jon to the cath lab and try to clear the blockage. He drew me a picture.

Questions and objections flew through my mind for the next few hours. Finally, the doctor rounded the corner.

"It went well. He should be okay."

He was okay, and he is okay. I write this chapter almost four years to the day since his heart attack. We have both changed. Jon works out even more, eats even better, and is much more conscious of controlling his stress levels. I'm a little more scared, and a little less carefree. And I understand damages a little more personally.

Everyone has their damages. Some you see, like a wheelchair, a breathing tube, a scar. But we all have scars that others can't see. In court, patients can be awarded money for pain, suffering, embarrassment, and the loss of life's pleasures. In life outside the courtroom, we often suffer those damages in silence. If we let them, our damages can make us stronger, better, and sometimes closer to others. The lessons I've learned from Jon's heart attack have made me more sensitive to others and more empathetic to the patients in my cases. If you know another way to learn about damages, go with it, because that was a trial I wouldn't wish on anyone. I also wouldn't trade it. Pain is often our best teacher.

PROVE IT

Many of us will experience a traumatic event of some type.[38] Research on victims of serious trauma has found that, for some survivors, there can actually be something called post-traumatic growth.[39] It may be true that what doesn't kill us makes us stronger.

SUMMARY OF THE CASE

1. Everyone has been hurt, and everyone is damaged in some way. Consider that as you weigh whether you need to go to battle.

2. When you go in for the kill, you leave scars behind. That damage may be worth it, or it may not. You have to be aware of the potential of damage in order to weigh the risks and benefits.

3. You, too, have your damages. Be gentle with yourself.

25

Close with Respect

"Dignity... means a belief in oneself, that one is worthy of the best. Dignity means that what I have to say is important, and I will say it when it's important for me to say it. Dignity really means that I deserve the best treatment I can receive. And that I have the responsibility to give the best treatment I can to other people."

MAYA ANGELOU

A T THE END of each trial, we lawyers shake hands. After years of conflict, arguments, and objections, our case is in the jury's hands. We've given our best in advocating for our clients, and there's nothing left to fight. Win or lose, we can leave one another with dignity and respect. I always shake an opponent's hand when the jury leaves to deliberate.

Sometimes my clients don't get it. They want me to reject the opponent, deny his dignity, and treat him like an enemy at all times. I understand. Oftentimes, showing the opponent respect isn't easy. I've had cases where I didn't like the other attorney. I didn't trust him, I resented her inability to cooperate,

I hated his tone. But I have to believe that each of those attorneys was doing the best job possible for her client, and I have to respect the fight itself.

For me, the courtroom is all about respect. I respect our system, and our judges. I respect the juries, and they know it. I've had jurors tell me they appreciated how much I respected their time and their attention. Even when I have to cross-examine injured patients with vigor, I respect them. I work hard never to take a witness' dignity even when I take their version of the truth. I have to show respect for the other side, because otherwise I'd lose respect for myself. And if in fighting the war, you lose self-respect—you lose your elegance—have you really won?

Whether you apply these lessons from lawsuits to the courtroom, the bedroom, or the boardroom, I hope you start and end with respect and dignity. When you refuse to respect others, whether you're ending a relationship or leaving a job, you take a piece of their dignity. And if you don't respect yourself, you lose a piece of your dignity. Finding it again takes time and effort that is better spent on other things.

PROVE IT

I was surprised by how little research there is on dignity and respect, especially since they are important to all of us. In one study of twenty thousand employees worldwide, respondents ranked respect as the most important leadership behavior. Yet they also reported more disrespectful behavior every year.[40] Respect and dignity are paramount, and we need to learn how to give and demand it.

SUMMARY OF THE CASE

1. If you win your trial but lose respect, your own or that of your opponents, the long-term result may be a loss.

2. When you respect yourself, others follow. Teach people how to treat you.

3. Put your best self forward. It makes giving and earning respect much easier.

26

Embrace Rejection

"Rejections puts you out of your comfort zone which is usually when you're at your best."

STEWART STAFFORD

I PACE AND DO crossword puzzles. Others go back to their office, talk on the phone, or eat hot dogs. Sometimes they eat too many hot dogs. I have one trial attorney friend who ate six hot dogs one afternoon while waiting for the jury to come back with a verdict.

Trials sometimes feel like hell. The sleepless nights, the conflict, and the pressure of a client depending on you can be like fire licking at your heels. Then the trial ends, and waiting for the verdict is purgatory. At the end of each trial, I've given every bit of myself to my client. I'm living on sleepless nights, too much coffee, and loads of adrenaline. Closings are done, and the minute they end, my knees buckle a bit. (Another reason to wear a pantsuit.) I used to think that the hard work would end with the closing, but the hard work has only just begun—now I have to wait for the jury to return a verdict, and patience is a virtue that passed me by. I strive to live and advocate with the 3Ps in mind, but there is a reason perfection is not one of the Ps. No one is perfect.

At the end of the case, the jury is given a verdict slip, legal instructions, and often lunch. Then they walk out of the courtroom, and the lawyers remain. We wait. The judges often let us leave the room, but we have to be close enough to return to the courtroom quickly. We may need to return because the jury has a verdict, but also because they have a question. Either way, they let the court officer know, and the court officer then lets the judge know. The judge calls the lawyers and the court reporter to the courtroom. Often, the court reporter is in another courtroom or back at her office, so we may have to wait for her. All this waiting, just to face the reality that someone in that courtroom is going to lose. Losing amounts to rejection, and rejection hurts.

While I've been fortunate enough to have won more cases than I've lost, I still feel the sting of rejection. By the time the trial is over, your case is part of you and the story you've told is inseparable from the person you are. And then the jury comes back and rejects that story. The pain from that rejection is real. Trial lawyers have to learn to shake it off. We have to be able to see that the jury is rejecting our case, our story, and our evidence, but not us. We have to be able to move on to the next case, ready for battle despite the loss.

You face rejection as well. There are times you won't get the job you want, the partner you want, or the life you want. But you do get to decide how you will see those losses. If you see them as a rejection of your skills, your love, your hope, then you will suffer. But if you see rejection as redirection, you can try again. Sometimes rejection is the greatest gift of all. I truly believe that what is meant for you will not pass you by. Remember that, especially during the waiting. If you don't get what you think you want, it may be that the wait for the right thing is just a little bit longer than you thought. Keep the faith, and the waiting becomes less painful.

Rejection is also our best teacher. I have learned more from the cases I've lost than I have from the cases I've won. I've learned what doesn't work, which leads me to what does. But most importantly, I've learned about myself. Lessons such as that I need time to cry when I'm hurt, because I have to feel it to heal it. And that I tend to stop taking care of myself when I feel rejected. I go to the pantry to eat my feelings, and I lie on the couch while they digest. Those lessons can make me better. I try to give myself time to cry when I'm hurt, and I try to go straight to the gym when I'm done crying. Try to let your losses leave you with lessons. The waiting and the pain all have value. Don't let it go to waste.

PROVE IT

There's a lot of research showing that rejection hurts.[41] It's an actual physical pain, as anyone who has ever had their heart broken knows all too well. We shouldn't underestimate the physical effect that rejection might have on us. Tylenol may help, but better connections and stronger communities may prevent the pain.

The negative impact of rejection doesn't stop with physical pain.[42] It can harm our spirits as well. Research on rejection is important because it will motivate us to move on from rejection, but will also help us realize that until we do, we may be a little less able to rely on our brains to help us out.

SUMMARY OF THE CASE

1. The waiting really is the hardest part. Use that time to take care of yourself—physically, mentally, and spiritually.

2. Remember that you are not being rejected. Your case, your argument, or your battle may have been lost; you are not.

3. Take the lesson you learned from this rejection and apply it. It may be just the lesson you need to win the next trial.

27

Quiet Your Lizard Brain

"The lizard brain is the source of the resistance."
SETH GODIN

IF YOU'VE DONE any reading on social psychology and the anatomy of the brain, you may know that some believe the reptile brain, which is responsible for our survival instincts, was the first part of the brain to develop. The reptile brain cares about life functions like eating and breathing, anything that's vital to your survival.

There are some lawyers who think jurors have lizard brains. Many patients' lawyers take classes in how to talk to that part of the brain. They learn how to use their case to establish a danger that the accused poses to the community, and therefore the jurors. Then they provide the jurors with the means to protect themselves—a verdict. It's manipulative, it underestimates jurors, but it often works.

The way lawyers do this is by tapping into jurors' fear. They tap into the need to be part of a group, or a tribe. They tap into hunger, the need for safety, and thirst. They use the lizard brain to win.

For example, I recently had a case where the doctor had failed to follow up on a study that had been ordered by another doctor. That doctor had allegedly failed to follow up on an X-ray report that showed a nodule on the lungs. He chose to settle with the patient. However, since the X-ray report was in the electronic medical record, the patient claimed that all of the doctors who saw the electronic medical record should have seen it and should have followed up on it. We disagreed. If every doctor is responsible for every piece of information in an electronic record, doctors would never be able to stop reviewing the record. They'd have no time to treat patients.

During trial, the patient's attorney used the lizard brain theory. Every time he had the opportunity, he referred to safety, to survival. He threw it into his opening, and during his closing he blatantly (and improperly) argued that the jurors couldn't let this happen to them or their family members. He told the jurors that someone needed to be held responsible. He tapped into their fear. The jurors disagreed, and we won that case. The lizard brain lost.

You have your fears, your personal lizard brain. Get to know it. The lizard brain is something you have to know to beat. So get familiar with what your lizard brain wants. It's hungry, it's thirsty, and it needs social support. It's scared. But then know this—you are not only that part of your brain. You've evolved. You have other parts of your brain, parts that are kind and compassionate and fun. You have parts of your brain that make you laugh, and use logic, and spread light. Sometimes it seems the world is trying to use our lizard brain to control us. The news, politicians, advertisers, and marketers all try to tap into the lizard brain to win. Don't let them.

I am well acquainted with my lizard brain. If I were to let my lizard brain rule, I'd believe that every trial was life or death. A loss would mean a loss of the means of survival. I'd be risking my job and thus the money it takes to feed my hungers and my thirsts. I'd be taking the risk that the tribe, the jury, would reject me. If my lizard brain ruled, I might never step into a courtroom. But I fight like hell to stop my lizard brain from taking over. While every trial becomes a part of my DNA, I remind myself that I am not my trials. I am the way I overcome them. I am the way I handle a loss. I am a friend to the clients I have grown to love. I am the fun I have with my team, the laughs we share, and the way I can be kind to opposing counsel even in the heat of battle.

Show your lizard brain who's boss. Show it that you have evolved beyond fear and you will take risks. You have evolved beyond hunger and you will feed more than your stomach. You've evolved beyond jealousy and you will include others. Your trials don't define you. Wins and losses mean nothing except for the lessons you've taken from each. Sometimes we learn more from our losses than our wins. And our lizard brain hasn't a clue about the value of those lessons.

Your lizard brain is there to protect you. It needs to know that it's safe, because then it will leave you be—it can take a bath in the sun, relaxed and at ease. No one but you is chasing you, and no one but you stands in your way. The biggest threat is no longer a predator, but rather the lies you tell yourself about perceived dangers. Stop telling them, stop believing them, and the threat goes away.

PROVE IT

If you're interested in lizard brain theory, there's plenty to read. In their book *Reptile: The 2009 Manual of the Plaintiff's Revolution*, David Ball and Don Keenan teach lawyers to persuade jurors by tapping into their lizard brains. In *Linchpin*, Seth Godin argues that we have to move beyond our lizard brains. Yet the brain is a little more complicated than these books would have us believe. In fact, the human brain is a unified whole, and our genes, experiences, and education are what help us make decisions.[43] Use every part of your brain if you want to win.

SUMMARY OF THE CASE

1. You can't win if you're too afraid to lose. Trade your survival instincts for a willingness to learn, and you're more likely to win.

2. You aren't your lizard brain; nor are you your wins or your losses. You are a combination of everything that ever happened to you, and to your ancestors. This win, or this loss, is just a small piece of that.

3. Let your lizard brain know that it is safe. It can rest and allow you to take the risks you need to take to win.

CONCLUSION

Win or Lose, Fight with Elegance

NO TRIALS, NO triumphs. If I hadn't tried so many cases, I wouldn't have so many wins. But I also wouldn't have learned so many life lessons in the courtroom without having both wins and losses. We need trials in life to keep us strong and open, and to show us what we've learned.

But trials have also wreaked havoc on my spirit and my well-being. I've had a lot of health issues in the last few years, and my doctors attribute them to years of living off cortisol and coffee. My best friend, who is also a trial lawyer, used to live in the same building as me. When I was on trial, she'd call to see what I needed. More often than I'd like to admit, my answer was "coffee." She'd leave ground coffee outside my door so as not to disturb me. It was our own destructive form of Meals on Wheels. My body and my mind have paid the price, and I'm tired.

As I write this, I've just finished a three-week trial, and I don't have another one scheduled for the rest of the year. This is a big change from past years, when I've tried up to seven complex medical cases in a year. I made a conscious decision to step back a little to think, write, and celebrate life. My experience reflects the things I think about. It took a case to teach me that as well.

I represented a hotshot young female resident. She was my age, and like me she was quickly rising in the ranks of a profession dominated by males and testosterone. She'd worked hard, and sacrificed sleep and fun to get where she was. She'd just taken a job she'd been working towards for her entire career. And now, we were going to trial. The case involved a young girl who'd died in the hospital after a swimming accident. My client was the doctor on call. She suspected there was something more going on than the accident, and had called in the appropriate consultants. The patient had died anyway, and the family's attorney claimed it was the fault of my client.

In Philadelphia, we pick juries on Fridays and start with openings on Monday mornings. My client was on call that weekend, so she wasn't at jury selection. While the parties don't have to be at jury selection, I do prefer that my clients come. The more the jury sees my client, the better. I called her on my walk home to fill her in on the jury makeup. She listened thoughtfully—she did everything thoughtfully. We discussed our defenses and finalized our plan to meet that Sunday to prep. Before we hung up, she added, "Heather, just so you know, my boss says I might lose this job if we lose this case. I need to talk to him further to really understand the ins and outs, but something about the board and my license or something. This case is really important to me and my family."

Every single case is important to me. But I was already a little overinvested in this one. She was young, like me. Driven, like me. A woman in a field of men, decisive, confident. She was also vulnerable as hell. And now this woman who had saved so many lives was looking to me to save her.

As we spoke, I could feel my lips swelling. One of the early signs that my hormones were rebelling against my lifestyle was hives. I get them when stressed, my body's reaction to the onslaught of cortisol. They usually limit themselves to my legs, specifically my upper thighs, my butt, and anywhere I have a scar. But not on this day. On this day, they limited themselves to the lips I planned to use to speak for this doctor.

By the time I reached my condo, my lips had exploded in size. I started to panic, and the anxiety made them worse. Hormones are an amazing thing. I began to feel like I couldn't swallow, then I felt like I couldn't breathe. I took a Benadryl, but there was no change. Finally, I decided to go to the hospital. I hoped I had time to get there via Uber, because I was too embarrassed to call an ambulance. The Uber driver kept nervously looking at my expanding lips in the rearview mirror. The minute the triage nurse saw me, she rushed me into the treatment area, and the steroids and IV Benadryl started. Right before I was set to argue the case involving a resident, I spent twenty hours in an emergency room surrounded by residents. Manifestation is real.

I made it out of the hospital in time to go straight to my expert's house to prepare him for his testimony. I was still swollen and exhausted, but was well enough to do my job. The case took two full weeks to try, so my client had to get a hotel room, and because the trial took longer than expected, she had to leave the minute closings were over—she couldn't stay while the jury deliberated. One of the biggest triumphs of my career was the call I made to her after days of jury deliberation. We had won.

That trial taught me what determination looked like. My client balanced childcare, the trial, her fear, and her career, finding a way to communicate to the jury effectively enough to win her case. It also taught me I had to find a way to invest a little less of myself in my cases. Learning how to do that has taken a little bit longer, and I still struggle. That was not my last trip to the ER during a trial. I'm still learning.

No trials, no triumphs. That is true. But I'm wondering if I have to continue to look for trials. They come in life, for all of us. My days of courting trials, stepping into the courtroom to actively seek them out, may be numbered. Or maybe it's just that I need a break. Either way, the lessons I've learned in the courtroom are my real triumphs. They make me who I am.

Another word for *trial* is *test*. In the courtroom, jurors test your case, but in the boardroom, the bedroom, the operating room, and beyond, life tests you. Whether it's a difficult client, an angry customer, a frustrated child, or an indifferent partner, every day has its trials, and you want to pass the test. You want to win the trial.

Trial lawyers win (or lose) by asking questions, and my question for you is, "How do you want to win?" Because how you win or lose may have more impact on your life than the outcome itself. And while outside factors may impact whether you celebrate victory or mourn defeat, the *how* is completely within your control. You can choose who you want to be.

I had a case with multiple defendants, and an opposing attorney who was very invested in winning. One day, at the end of court, we had all begun to pack up our things, put away our binders, and head home for a few hours of sleep. My trials are document heavy, as they involve huge amounts of medical records and medical literature. Exhibits are everywhere, and the attorneys' notebooks are often scattered among their boxes, marked with their names and their firms' names. I left the courtroom, but quickly turned around and came back to grab my umbrella. There, I saw the opposing attorney rooting through the boxes on my side of the room. When I cleared my throat, he jumped and tried to pretend he was looking for a pen. He wasn't. He was looking for an advantage, and he may have found one in that box. When we all shook hands at the end of the trial, he was unable to meet my eye. I'd lost respect for him, but even more tragically, he'd lost respect for himself.

I choose not to practice that way and not to live that way. I always want to be proud to make eye contact, whether it be with counsel, my client, or myself in the mirror.

Many attorneys opt to live their lives in doubt. I know one attorney who has his associate pack up every one of his boxes every day, in every trial. Even in cases where the other attorneys don't give him any reason to be suspicious, he wheels out boxes and boxes of exhibits every afternoon and wheels them back in every morning. I choose not to live that way either. I've come up with a compromise that works for me. At the end of each day, I pack up my boxes and put them in a pile. Then I change out of my high heels and into my sneakers, placing the high heels on the very top of the closed boxes. My version of elegance means protecting my work, but not to the point of paranoia. It means leaving the courtroom with my stilettos as a sentry. For me, elegance is walking home in my sneakers, and sometimes even singing.

Notes

1. Robert M. Sapolsky, "Why Stress Is Bad for Your Brain." *Science* 273, no. 5276 (1996): 749–750. Available at science.sciencemag.org/content/273/5276/749.

2. Michael Kraus and Wendy Berry Mendes, "Sartorial Symbols of Social Class Elicit Class-Consistent Behavior and Physiological Responses: A Dyadic Approach." *Journal of Experimental Psychology, General* 143, no. 6 (2014): 2330–2340. Available at www.ncbi.nlm.nih.gov/pubmed/25222264.

3. Hajo Adam and Adam D. Galinsky, "Enclothed Cognition." *Journal of Experimental Social Psychology* 8, no. 4 (July 2012): 918–925. Available at www.sciencedirect.com/science/article/pii/S0022103112000200#!.

4. Silvia Bellezza, Francesca Gino, and Anat Keinan, "The Red Sneakers Effect: Inferring Status and Competence from Signals of Nonconformity." *Journal of Consumer Research* 41 (June 2014): 35–54. Available at hbs.edu/faculty/Publication%20Files/The%20Red%20Sneakers%20Effect%20 2014_4657b733-84f0-4ed6-a441-d401bbbac19d.pdf

5. Karen Huang et al., "It Doesn't Hurt to Ask: Question-Asking Increases Liking." *Journal of Personality and Social Psychology* 113, no. 3 (2017): 430–452. Available at hbs.edu/faculty/Publication%20Files/Huang%20et%20 al%202017_6945bc5e-3b3e-4c0a-addd-254c9e603c60.pdf.

6. John Dunlosky et al., "Improving Students' Learning with Effective Learning Techniques." *Psychological Science in the Public Interest* 14, no. 1 (2013): 4–58. Available at indiana.edu/~pcl/rgoldsto/courses/dunloskyimprovinglearning .pdf.

7. Kathleen A. Lawler et al., "The Unique Effects of Forgiveness on Health: An Exploration of Pathways." *Journal of Behavioral Medicine* 28, no. 2 (April 2005): 157–167. Available at link.springer.com/article/10.1007/ s10865-005-3665-2.

8. Maya Tamir and Yochanan E. Bigman, "Expectations Influence How Emotions Shape Behavior." *Emotion* 18, no. 1 (2018): 15–25. Available at psycnet.apa.org/doiLanding?doi=10.1037%2Femo0000351.

9. Monica C. Higgins and David A. Thomas, "Constellations and Careers: Toward Understanding the Effects of Multiple Developmental Relationships." *Journal of Organizational Behavior* 22, no. 33 (May 2001): 223–247. Available at https://onlinelibrary.wiley.com/doi/abs/10.1002/job.66.

10. Rajaji Ghosh and Thomas G. Reio Jr. "Career Benefits Associated with Mentoring for Mentors: A Meta-Analysis. *Journal of Vocational Behavior* 83, no. 1 (August 2013): 106–116. Available at sciencedirect.com/science/article/abs/pii/S0001879113001012.

11. Mayo Clinic Staff, "Stress Relief from Laughter? It's No Joke." Mayo Clinic, April 21, 2016. Available at mayoclinic.org/healthy-lifestyle/stress-management/in-depth/stress-relief/art-20044456.

12. Zak Stambor, "How Laughing Leads to Learning." *Monitor on Psychology* 37, no. 6 (June 2006): 62. Available at apa.org/monitor/jun06/learning.aspx.

13. Benjamin Artz, Amanda Goodall, and Andrew J. Oswald, "Research: Women Ask for Raises as Often as Men, but Are Less Likely to Get Them. *Harvard Business Review*, June 25, 2018. Available at hbr.org/2018/06/research-women-ask-for-raises-as-often-as-men-but-are-less-likely-to-get-them.

14. Simone M. Ritter and Ap Dijksterhuis, "Creativity—the Unconscious Foundations of the Incubation Period." *Frontiers in Human Neuroscience* 8, no. 215 (April 11, 2014). Available at ncbi.nlm.nih.gov/pmc/articles/PMC3990058.

15. Amy C. Edmondson, "Managing the Risk of Learning: Psychological Safety in Work Teams." In *International Handbook of Organizational Teamwork and Cooperative Working*, edited by Michael A. West, Dean Tjosvold, and Ken G. Smith, 255–276. London: Blackwell, 2003. Available at hbs.edu/faculty/Publication%20Files/02-062_0b5726a8-443d-4629-9e75-736679b870fc.pdf.

16. Julia Rozovsky, "The Five Keys to a Successful Google Team." *re:Work*, November 17, 2015. Available at rework.withgoogle.com/blog/five-keys-to-a-successful-google-team.

17. Simone Schnall, Kent D. Harber, Jeanine K. Stefanucci, and Dennis R. Proffitt. "Social Support and the Perception of Geographical Slant." *Journal of Experimental Social Psychology* 44, no. 5 (September 2008): 1246–1255. Available at sciencedirect.com/science/article/pii/S002210310800070X.

18. Randall L. Kiser, Martin A. Asher, and Blakely B. McShane, "Let's Not Make a Deal: An Empirical Study of Decision Making in Unsuccessful Settlement Negotiations." *Journal of Empirical Legal Studies* 5, no. 3 (September 2008): 552–591. Available at onlinelibrary.wiley.com/doi/full/10.1111/j.1740-1461.2008.00133.x.

19. J. Steven Picou, "When the Solution Becomes the Problem: The Impacts of Adversarial Litigation on Survivors of the *Exxon Valdez* Oil Spill." *University of St. Thomas Law Journal* 7, no. 1 (Fall 2009): Article 5. Available at researchgate.net/publication/254713536_When_the_Solution_Becomes_the_ Problem_The_Impacts_of_Adversarial_Litigation_on_Survivors_of_the_Exxon_ Valdez_Oil_Spill.

20. Mike Nudelman. "10 Proven Tactics for Reading People's Body Language." Business Insider, May 12, 2015. Available at businessinsider.com/10-tactics-for-reading-peoples-body-language-2015-5.

21. Michael W. Kraus. "Voice-Only Communication Enhances Empathic Accuracy." *American Psychologist* 72, no. 7 (2017): 644-654. Available at https://www.apa.org/pubs/journals/releases/amp-amp0000147.pdf.

22. Gretchen M. Spreitzer and Scott Sonenshein, "Toward the Construct Definition of Positive Deviance." *American Behavioral Scientist*, February 1, 2004. Available at journals.sagepub.com/doi/abs/10.1177/ 0002764203260212.

23. E. Tulving, "On the Law of Primacy." In *Memory and Mind: A Festschrift for Gordon H. Bower*, edited by Mark A. Gluck, John R. Anderson, and Stephen M. Kosslyn, 31-48. Mahwah, NJ: Lawrence Erlbaum Associates Publishers, 2008.

24. Susan Birch et al., "A 'Curse of Knowledge' in the Absence of Knowledge? People Misattribute Fluency When Judging How Common Knowledge Is Among Their Peers." *Cognition* 166 (2017): 447-458. Available at ncbi.nlm .nih.gov/pubmed/28641221.

25. Karen Huang et al., "It Doesn't Hurt to Ask."

26. Tal Eyal, Mary Steffel, and Nicholas Epley, "Perspective Mistaking: Accurately Understanding the Mind of Another Requires Getting Perspective, Not Taking Perspective." *Journal of Personality and Social Psychology*, 114, no. 4 (2018): 547-571. Available at faculty.chicagobooth.edu/nicholas.epley/ Eyal_Steffel_Epley_2018_Perspective_Mistaking.pdf.

27. Karen Huang et al., "It Doesn't Hurt to Ask."

28. Albert Mehrabian and Morton Wiener, "Decoding of Inconsistent Communication." *Journal of Personality and Social Psychology* 6, no. 1 (1967): 109-114. Available at psycnet.apa.org/record/1967-08861-001.

29. Jocelyn A. Sze et al., "Coherence Between Emotional Experience and Physiology: Does Body Awareness Training Have an Impact?" *Emotion* 10, no. 6 (December 2010): 803-814. Available at ncbi.nlm.nih.gov/pmc/ articles/PMC4175373.

30. Paul J. Zak, "The Neuroscience of Trust." *Harvard Business Review*, January-February 2017. Available at hbr.org/2017/01/the-neuroscience-of-trust.

31. Kevin Jon Heller, "The Cognitive Psychology of Circumstantial Evidence." *Michigan Law Review* 105 (2006): 241-306. Available at papers.ssrn.com/ sol3/papers.cfm?abstract_id=891695.

32. Amy Cuddy, "Your Body Language May Shape Who You Are." TEDGlobal 2012 video, 20:56, June 2012. Available at ted.com/talks/amy_cuddy_your_body_language_shapes_who_you_are?language=en.

33. Amy Cuddy, *Presence: Bringing Your Boldest Self to Your Biggest Challenges.* Columbus, Georgia: Little, Brown and Company, 2015.

34. Adam G. Galinsky and Li Huang, "How You Can Become More Powerful by Literally Standing Tall." *Scientific American*, January 4, 2011. Available at scientificamerican.com/article/how-you-can-become-more-p.

35. Michèle Lamont and Virág Molnár, "The Study of Boundaries in the Social Sciences." *Annual Review of Sociology* 28 (August 2002): 167-195. Available at annualreviews.org/doi/abs/10.1146/annurev.soc.28.110601.141107.

36. Tara Sophia Mohr, "Why Women Don't Apply for Jobs Unless They're 100% Qualified." *Harvard Business Review*, August 25, 2014. Available at hbr.org/2014/08/why-women-dont-apply-for-jobs-unless-theyre-100-qualified.

37. Kate Kershner, "What's the Baader-Meinhof Phenomenon?" HowStuffWorks, March 20, 2015. Available at science.howstuffworks.com/life/inside-the-mind/human-brain/baader-meinhof-phenomenon.htm.

38. Fran H. Norris, "Epidemiology of Trauma: Frequency and Impact of Different Potentially Traumatic Events on Different Demographic Groups." *Journal of Consulting and Clinical Psychology* 60, no. 3 (July 1992): 409-418. Available at researchgate.net/publication/21536828_Epidemiology_of_Trauma_Frequency_and_Impact_of_Different_Potentially_Traumatic_Events_on_Different_Demographic_Groups.

39. Ibid.

40. Kristie Rogers, "Do Your Employees Feel Respected?" *Harvard Business Review*, July–August 2018. Available at hbr.org/2018/07/do-your-employees-feel-respected.

41. Ethan Kross et al., "Social Rejection Shares Somatosensory Representations with Physical Pain." *Proceedings of the National Academy of Sciences of the United States of America* 108, no. 15 (2011): 6270–6275. Available at ncbi.nlm.nih.gov/pmc/articles/PMC3076808.

42. Roy Baumeister, Jean M. Twenge, and Christopher K. Nuss, "Effects of Social Exclusion on Cognitive Processes: Anticipated Aloneness Reduces Intelligent Thought." *Journal of Personality and Social Psychology* 83, no. 4 (October 2002): 817-827. Available at ncbi.nlm.nih.gov/pubmed/12374437.

43. Ben Thomas, "Revenge of the Lizard Brain." *Scientific American*, September 7, 2012. Available at blogs.scientificamerican.com/guest-blog/revenge-of-the-lizard-brain.

Acknowledgments

I'D LIKE to thank my family, Mum, Dad, Jess, Brian, and Phil for your support, honesty, and your love. I know how lucky I am. I'd like to thank my sister-in-law, Jaime, for her guidance. Only someone who has written a book can know the gremlins, and she helped me fight them. Thank you to Jon Leiberman—your support made this book happen. Thanks to Judge Moss and Judge Aquilina for letting me tell a little piece of their stories. And thanks to Deb Lorber, who gave me my first courtroom yes. I'd also like to thank Christine Guiliano for the Meals on Wheels and for the wind beneath my wings.

Huge thanks to the team at Page Two, who made this process easy and, dare I say it, fun. Amanda, you made the book much better without making me feel less. You are so good at what you do. Finally, thanks to my partners at O'Brien and Ryan, especially John O'Brien and Dan Ryan. You taught me as much about life as you did about the law, and those lessons are forever a part of me.

About the Author

HEATHER HANSEN IS a trial lawyer. She has defended medical malpractice cases for over twenty years, was recently inducted into the American College of Trial Lawyers, and is consistently named one of the Top 50 female attorneys in the state of Pennsylvania. Heather works as a communication consultant, combining her courtroom experience with her psychology degree and her training as a mediator to help her clients ask better questions, master objections, and use credible persuasion to succeed. She has appeared on CNN, NBC, Fox News Channel, and *Good Day Philadelphia*, and is the host of *The Elegant Warrior* podcast. Heather Hansen lives in New York City.

www.heatherhansenpresents.com